ROUGH WEATHER
MAKES GOOD TIMBER

ROUGH WEATHER
MAKES GOOD TIMBER

Carolinians Recall

by Patsy Moore Ginns

J. L. Osborne, Jr., Artist

The University of North Carolina Press / Chapel Hill

© 1977 The University of North Carolina Press
All rights reserved
Manufactured in the United States of America
Cloth edition, published 1977, ISBN 0-8078-1288-9
Paper edition, published 1980, ISBN 0-8078-4071-8
Library of Congress Catalog Card Number 76-20765

First printing, April 1977
Second printing, November 1977
Third printing, January 1979
Fourth printing, August 1980
Fifth printing, August 1984

Library of Congress Cataloging in Publication Data
Main entry under title:

Rough weather makes good timber.

 Edited transcripts of tape-recorded interviews.
 1. North Carolina—Social life and customs.
2. Country life—North Carolina. I. Ginns, Patsy
Moore. II. Osborne, Jesse Lee, 1923–
F259.R68 975.6 76-20765
ISBN 0-8078-1288-9

CONTENTS

ILLUSTRATIONS

PREFACE

This book was written by the people of rural North Carolina. The words are their words; the pictures are of places that reflect their lives.

Mr. Osborne and I are honored to have been the instruments by which their scenes and accounts have been recorded.

When we decided to compile a book on rural life in North Carolina in an earlier day, we felt the primary source of authentic information would be the people themselves, those who had lived through those years and could recount them firsthand.

We were not disappointed. While Mr. Osborne set about his travels to seek out places he felt to be truly representative of ordinary everyday life, I began my visits into the homes of older people.

Both of us were received with genuine hospitality and an eager willingness to assist the project in every possible way. I was made to feel at home in each county I visited and even on board *The Pamlico*, a ferry running between Cedar Island and Ocracoke, as Captain Floyd Daniels recounted for me his impressions of earlier times.

Everywhere, friends and acquaintances introduced me to those they felt would have valuable accounts to offer. Librarians and teachers, especially, offered the project a helping hand. To each of these persons we owe a debt of gratitude that can only be repaid by the sharing of the material itself.

And now, what of those persons whose words are recorded here? First of all, they are North Carolinians, practically all native to the state, and, with few exceptions, of retirement age and older. The oldest person I interviewed was ninety-seven at the time; the youngest, fifty-three.

In every instance, they shared their accounts with a sincerity bordering on reverence as they recalled, often in astonishing detail, life as they had known it. Consequently, we see here a life style reported honestly and genuinely. Older people are prone to leave off the "whitewashing"; thus, they tell of a simple, straightforward existence, often bleak, sometimes touching and heartwarming, at times humorous, but nearly always honest.

The words were recorded verbatim by means of a tape recorder and with a minimum of editing. In certain cases I have substituted fictitious names for real ones given within the accounts in order to respect the privacy of those persons still living or who may have existent relatives. In other cases the narrator seemed to prefer having real names used. Always the narrator's name, age, and county is authentic.

In an effort to facilitate the appreciation of singular phrases and provide easy reading, I have written many passages in free-form poetic scans. These, too, are verbatim.

We have attempted to maintain no geographic or chronological order. The earliest first-hand accounts go back to around 1885, and the latest ones reach into the post-Depression era. However, in the final chapter certain accounts go back into Revolutionary times. In these cases, the stories and legends have been preserved in families, for the most part, and are often recorded here for the first time.

At times the words and pictures are specifically meant for each other. In general, however, they only blend in feeling.

And so here in a package is a sampling of the cultural heritage of North Carolina, which its people have preserved for themselves.

ROUGH WEATHER
MAKES GOOD TIMBER

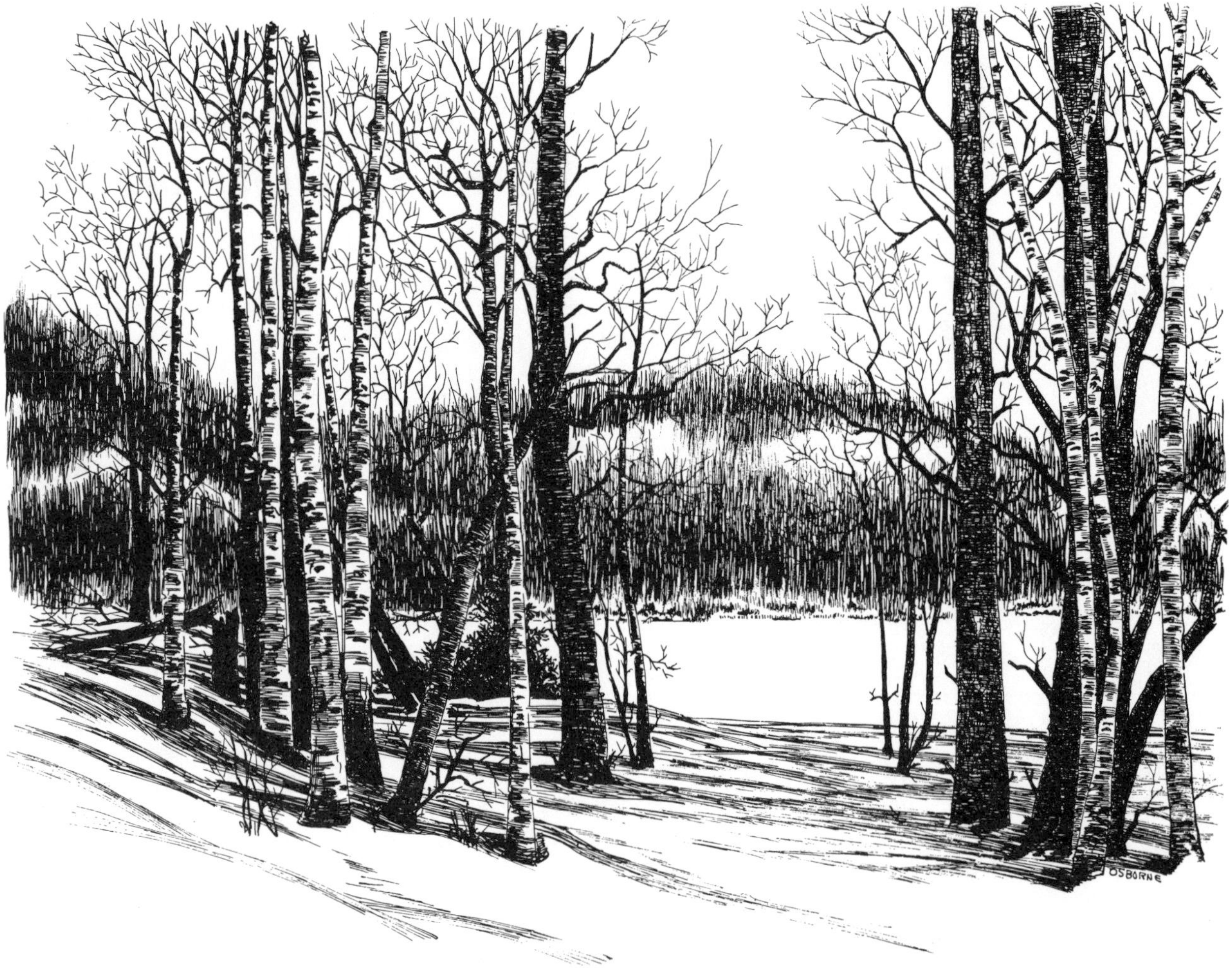
OSBORNE

1 THE LAND

During the years that spanned the turn of the century, people of rural North Carolina lived close to their land. At times the soil itself settled the matter of survival for a mountain family. Through unfaltering faith in their land and themselves, these people resolutely lived in harmony with the seasons, sometimes in joyous celebration of their land, sometimes in spite of it.

We Had Everything

I am one of eleven children.
I was born at Air Bellows.
Three miles south of Whitehead.

We was born right on top
of the Blue Ridge Mountain.
My father's farm
run right along where the Scenic is now.

We enjoyed it.
We had everything.
We had outdoors and we had the streams,
and we had all the beauty of God's creation.

We enjoyed it so much.

NORA C. WAGONER, 1882
Alleghany County

A Mountain Farm

My father bought that mountain farm, and he and my mother married. There wasn't a stick of it missing, I guess. And he just put him up a little house about as big as this room, just big enough for two beds, cupboard in one corner and a table in the middle of the floor with shelves on the other side for pots and pans and things.

My mother never owned a cook stove. She cooked over the fire.

So Daddy was fixing to build him a new house. He just built him a little cabin till he could clear some and get started. Just built it to be for the stock when he got a bigger, better house built. Well, he was cutting and logging for his bigger house, him and his neighbor. His neighbor had married a little earlier, but they were working and logging together to build them both a new house apiece.

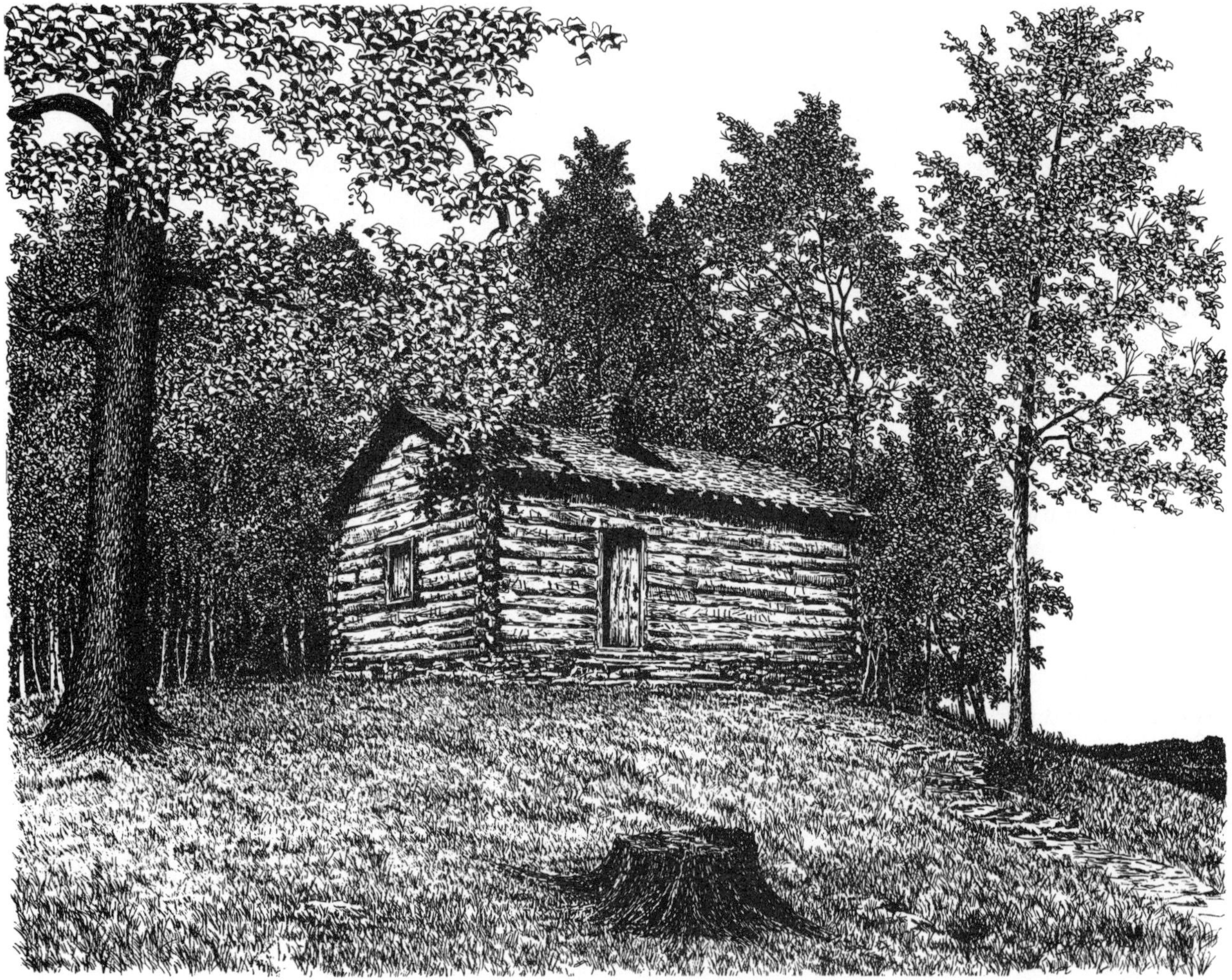

And poor old Daddy, he had him a pack of lumber; and when he got cut and died, you know, Mother had to sell that lumber. She couldn't go no further with it, to build it. And I guess we lived in that little log house for about twenty years.

When Daddy died, I wasn't six years old till February. He died in November. I wasn't six years old; my brother, four; my sister, two.

And the next spring my mother put us to helping her hoe corn. And my brother, he was so little . . . and I'd get behind, but she'd help us up. But we took our row of corn. But she stayed right there on that mountain and raised us up till we all left. And my brother went to Piney Creek, and she went to Piney Creek with him.

But we kept the old farm till a year or two ago. But I went up there last fall. My nephew took me up there. And the old graves were gone, and it looked so bad I wished I hadn't seen it. Couldn't see where the spring was, where the meadow was, or anything. Just gone back to woods, nearly. But it didn't seem like old home.

But I want to tell you about the loom business. My mother, she carded and spun. She'd take the wool off'n the sheep's back and card it and spin it, you know. Wove all our clothes. She made all her clothes. Never owned a sewing machine in her life. She had an awful tough time.

But Mother sold more corn than ever she bought. She had two kinds of corn she planted. She called one of them "white" and the other "hominy corn." And we'd shell half a bushel, all three of us. And your hands would be blistered, it was so hard to shell.

Well, when me and my brother got big enough to go to mill, she'd put us a peck of corn in a sack and send us to mill. She could do more work on the farm than we could, you know. She'd send us to mill, and one old man who lived there close would get there early in the morning before we did, and it might be twelve o'clock before we'd get back home with the meal. And sometimes, we just had to leave it. They just had a little pond, you know, and a little water wheel. And in dry weather that little pond wouldn't fill up. So we had a time of it.

But we made it on Irish potatoes at home. Irish potatoes and soup beans and green beans and corn and cabbage and such as that. And then we got an orchard. 'Course, we had to have an orchard set out after Daddy died. He had the bed of sprouts, and we set them out. But it was ten years before we got so we could have anything much off of them. But we had a mighty good neighbor.

And Mother dried sweet fruit, you know. A bushel of sweet fruit. Sweet apples. We still dry sweet apples now.

But we lived on Irish potatoes and sweet fruit and beans and cabbage in the winter. And we never had no flour but buckwheat flour and rye flour. We'd sow rye in the fall of the year. Then the next July we'd start harvesting that rye, you know. And thresh it and take it to that mill, and it'd be black flour, just real dark flour.

How'd we thresh it? Lord-o'-mercy, it was a job! We started like we were going to build a rail pen; then we floored it with rails. And we'd take a stick about seven feet long and we'd beat it, just beat it thataway till we busted it all up.

Then we'd take the rails off, and there it was. But sometimes, if the wind wasn't blowing much, we'd have to take a sheet and bounce it up in the air and let the wind blow the chaff out. That's the way we done it! And it was the way we did for most of the bread we had—flour bread. Rye bread and buckwheat bread. But we loved buckwheat pancakes.

And, another thing: through the winter we had mush. Mother had a little oven, a little cast oven, and she'd put it on the fire and put in water, salt that water and make cornmeal mush. Then she'd set it on the hearth, and we each had our cups of milk. We'd sit around that oven, all four of us, and we'd take our spoons and dip it. We'd eat right by the fire when it was cold.

But, Lord-o'-mercy, you don't know nothing about cold times like we used to have back in them mountains. We'd eat by the fire and have mush. Mush just about every supper.

That little oven was a black iron pot with three legs to it, just straight up. We didn't use no lid when we made mush. Just got the water to boiling and stirred it in. And we took a corn stalk to stir that mush with. They said it made it better to stir it with a corn stalk.

And, a many a time, when we finished our supper and went to clean off the table, we'd just have to clean it off with a dry rag. We couldn't use no wet dishcloth; it'd freeze to the table. And, the more you'd try to wash it off, the more it'd freeze. So we just used a dry rag.

And my mother, when she'd get up every morning—she set her water buckets on the hearth, had to carry water far as from here over to that road, nearly—well, she'd set her buckets on the hearth, and the next morning she'd have to take the hammer and bust the ice because the water would be frozen so thick. And it right on the hearth, now, by the fireplace.

But she'd have four or five heavy quilts on us. Slept on a blanket and slept under a blanket.

Law me, folks don't know nothing about hard times now, do they?

And, in the wintertime it'd snow, you know, and we'd have to carry water. And if we were washing and it had snowed a big snow, we had a wash pot, and we'd carry in snow and put it in that pot and melt it. And if it come a big snow, upstairs—'course, it wasn't an upstairs, it was a loft—it'd snow in. We'd have to get up there and sweep it up, or it'd commence melting and running down on our beds. And many a morning Mother would have to get up and shake the snow off'n the quilts.

Oh, I had the best mother in the world, I reckon. I heard her tell people that when we were little and Daddy died and left her there with us, she didn't see no way to live and get along with us, but she did it.

MARTHA TOLIVER ABSHER, 1878
Alleghany County

The Sauratown Mountains

I've always been crazy about our mountains;
and when I was just a boy,
I used to climb our Sauratown Mountains,
which, you know,
begin and end in Stokes County.

I don't think there is any other county
in North Carolina that can brag of that.

Our Sauratown Mountains begin and end
within the county itself.

And just north of Yadkin Township
we have the White Walls,
as the rock cliffs there are called.
The White Walls.

To me that is a wonderful piece of scenery.
Yes, I've been in love with this mountain area.

R. HOLTON GENTRY, 1909
Stokes County

The Price of Land

There were some times,
I've heard
my pappy tell about,

that they could buy
land
for fifty cents
an
acre.

Maybe it was back
during
the War Between the States.

I've heard tell of it.

My granddaddy bought
hundreds of acres
and
settled all his boys
down on it.

Why, we bought
a lot of ours
for ten dollars
an acre.

MINNIE LEE SPENCER, 1879
Stokes County

When Tractors Came

When
the tractors
came in,
Mother
always said
the land
looked as though
it had been "washed and ironed,"

and
my grandmother
would
say,
"Yes, and starched."

LOUISE V. BOONE, 1922
Hertford County

North Carolina

I was born in North Carolina
and I've lived here all my life.
We've got the finest state there is.
We join the seacoast,
and we've got the mountains.
We have snow and sleet,
summer,
rain
and spring.

It's such a pretty time.

The winds blowing in March.
You know,
old Miss Wiltshire over yonder
used to say that the winds of March
just a-blowing the limbs of the trees
this way and that way—
she said that was just like cultivating your plants.
She said it exercises 'em,
causes the sap to start rising.
Just like cultivating your garden.
Makes 'em stretch out their limbs and grow!

And the fall.
I can look out my doorway in the fall,
look up toward the mountains.
Just about every color there is.

Yes, North Carolina's the best one yet.

LELIA F. BAKER, 1903
Stokes County

My Cousin's Land

I had
a
cousin
who had
a piece of land
that was not
the best
farming land in the world.

And she said,
"It
was
so
poor
you
couldn't even raise hell on it."

LOUISE V. BOONE, 1922
Hertford County

2 HOME LIFE

All life centered closely around home and the family fireside in those early days. Both children and parents took evident pride in the self-sufficiency and ingenuity with which they met their own needs. Moral and family values were strong, and the youngsters depended upon their parents for much of their basic education. Material possessions were necessarily utilitarian, rather than aesthetic. But the gracious touch was not lacking. While flour sacks became delicately hemmed tea towels, simple honeysuckle found its way into fireplaces which had been freshly scrubbed and whitewashed for summer.

Feather Beds

When I was growing up,
we had a bed tick stuffed with straw
with a feather bed on
top of that.
In the morning,
you turned that feather bed down
and ruffled up the straw.
Then you turned the feather bed back up
and fluffed up the feathers.
Then you straightened the sheets
and bed quilts.
We didn't have blankets then,
just quilts.

And we had feather pillows.

In the spring of the year,
we'd pick the gray ducks.
We'd pick the soft gray feathers
on the breast
and back of the neck
to use
in our feather beds
and
pillows.

LUCY SPENCER, 1912
Stokes County

Our Home

Well, we just had us a little log cabin. It set right here just like this house does. We had two parts to it. The kitchen was separate. But we had the roof—or a shelter—that ran over the top between the two, and right in the middle was a dirt floor, and we kept it swept real clean. That's where we sat in the summer time and rested.

Windows? Well, we didn't have any windows then. But in the house there was a space about a yard long between the logs where we had a small log set so we could pull it out on one end, just swing it right open and let the air in—and the light, too. And then we'd close it back up. It was right in with the chinkin'.

Inside, we used kerosene lamps that we set on the table. And then we had lanterns that we carried around with us wherever we went. Then, too, we used torches in the fireplace. We would lay them right down on the front of the fireplace or stick the light'ard up in a crack between the rocks in the side of the fireplace.

Our fireplace was about a yard wide. It was the best old fireplace! Oh, I just loved to sit around it and bake ash cakes. We used to have the best ash cakes. They was so good. My mammy had clean rocks that she kept down in the fireplace, out in front, and she'd wipe them off and put the cornmeal dough right down on them in a little flat cake. Then she'd cover them up with hot embers. And they would bake. When the embers died down, she'd rake those back in the fireplace and get some hot ones.

And then, when they got all done, she'd take them up and they'd be so brown and hard and good. Then she'd take them to her pan of water and wash them, and that was the best corn bread you nearly ever tasted. No, they didn't get soggy. They was hard on the outside, and you could just wash the ashes right off, then dry them. They was good!

We didn't have no stove atall. Nobody around did. We cooked on the fireplace. I had my big old iron pot, but if we had something big to cook, then we put the washpot up in front of the fireplace and raked the coals out under it right on the hearth. Sometimes we'd boil a ham that way.

We got a stove about the time I got grown. My pappy bought one for us when they came around selling stoves. It was a nice one. Black iron. It had four cappers on top and a big door to bake in. And then later they started selling ranges.

MINNIE LEE SPENCER, 1879
Stokes County

My Mother

But I know
my mother always seemed to have the time.
And you never did
see her come out on the porch
in the afternoon,
but she would be dressed up.
And she never did come out
on the porch without having some little handwork.

And it was just a wonderful way—
not to sit there and hold your hands.

And my mother always wore aprons.
There'd always be a fresh white apron
over her dress.

The last pictures I have taken
of my mother
was sitting on the porch
with her apron on
and something in her hand.

MARY C. MC KINNON, 1886
Scotland County

Gathering Herbs

In the summer time we gathered up herbs for the winter. We used ginseng, squaw weed, wild cherry bark. The wild cherry was for the blood and the stomach; the squaw weed was for the bowels; the ginseng was for little children that had croup and diphtheria.

That ginseng grows right up here next to our neighbor's. It's the prettiest weed you nearly ever saw a-growing. And we gathered boneset, catnip, and horehound. Horehound was for coughs, boneset was for aches and pains, and catnip was awful good for pains, and it would make you sleep.

The boneset tea was awful bitter, but the catnip was pretty good. I expect the boneset is up now.

Then for colds and congestion, we used mutton tallow, turpentine, and camphor. Make a salve out of that tallow, grease their chest, between their shoulders, and the bottoms of their feet and the palms of their hands.

We have a boy who has been greased all over many a time with polecat grease. Had the croup. Had a neighbor woman who kept it, and she came over when we needed her. But, Lord-a-mercy, it stunk so bad! But I'd wash our little boy's shirts just as good as I could. We'd take the fat and fry it and get out the grease.

But her name was Zella, and when that boy would take the croup, I'd holler for her. We were in hollering distance. And she'd come running with her polecat-grease bottle in her hand. And she'd grease him on his chest, between his shoulders, under his arms, the palms of his hands, and the bottoms of his feet. She'd just about grease him all over. He was just a little feller. We thought we were going to lose him there for about three or four years. Every time he took a little cold, he'd take a spell of the croup. But we pulled him through.

MARTHA TOLIVER ABSHER, 1878
Alleghany County

Making Medicine

And we made
some of our own medicine,
like cough medicine for children.
The doctor told me
my teas were better for children
than his medicine,
because they weren't so strong.

I made all kinds of teas,
and, if they got a cold,
I'd fry a cloth
for their breast.

I'd fry it
in camphor
or mutton tallow
or something,
like he told me to,
and
pin it
inside their clothes
next
to
their breast.

MINNIE LEE SPENCER, 1879
Stokes County

Our Home on the Blue Ridge

It was pretty cold in the wintertime, but we had warm clothes. My mother made 'em herself, you know. She had a loom. And I have a piece of blanket that I helped weave myself. She let me weave, too.

We used yarn thread, and the warp was cotton. Cotton thread. The filling was wool. And the shuttle went back and forth. And that carried the wool thread. Then she had something to batter it closer. To make it tight.

I was about fourteen when my mother taught me to do that.

And she'd go out in the woods and get white oak bark. She'd take the inside out, you know. She'd take the rough part out and she'd skin that. And then she'd skin the maple.

And she'd boil those up together. And she'd go and get walnut roots. Then she'd take the bark off them and boil that. And this oak bark and everything was an astringent. And that would make it a fast color, kind of.

And it made it brown. Very brown. And after she would boil this and strain all the bark out and had the fluid, she put her copperas in, and that would set it. And she'd boil that all up together; then she'd put the yarn in. But she'd have to cool it first, you know. You couldn't put wool in hot water. You can't boil yarn, you know. It'll shrink and ruin it. And then she'd put that in and keep it in a long time, keep stirring it around so it'd be an even color, you see.

Now, that was after the yarn was made into little hanks. You've seen . . . skeins, they call it. And she'd make it into that, and that was colored, you know. And then she'd take that out and wash it and dry it.

And that was put onto the little quills, the spinning wheel. There was a quill that went on the spinner. And the yarn was rolled onto that, and that was put into the shuttle. It carried the thread back and forth in the loom.

We had warm brown linsey dresses. And that is what we wore at home and to school. In the wintertime.

I wish I had my spinning wheel here. I had one. Well, anyway, there's a spindle. Now, we had the large wheel that went around. And the spindle was on up here, you know. And Mother had quills, they called them quills, that were put on to run the yarn on. And this quill fitted into the shuttle.

My mother had her yarn in a ball, and she held onto it and fed it—let it run even, you know. She kept running it back and forth. You can't let it run all in one place. You have to keep it even. Like a bobbin on a sewing machine.

My daddy had sheep. And, too, we'd get the wool and get it made into long bats—rolls.

And the bats were larger than my thumb, and
about this long [measures].

And that was fastened onto this spindle on
the wheel. There's no quill put on that. And she'd
turn the wheel, and it'd twist that and make it into
yarn.

NORA C. WAGONER, 1882
Alleghany County

Making Underclothing

Those were the days when women wore clothes.
My mother would make, they'd call 'em
drawers and drawer-bodices.
You know, with buttons around the bottom
and then make these drawers.
You could pull 'em down and
pull 'em up.
Button 'em to the top.
We didn't wear nothing else under that.

Then sometimes, too, we wore union suits.
Like a man's underwear.
We didn't have no coat to wear;
we just wore a little cape or something.
What Mother had made for us.

We'd wear three or four petticoats
starched just as stiff.
There'd just be round holes for the arms
and a round neck.
Some would be full, and some wouldn't.
White cotton. Heavy.
What you lined quilts with.
That's what they used.
Sheeting.

MAGGIE JEFFERS, 1894
ETHEL LUTZ, 1898
Cleveland County

Dressmaking

I used to buy eight yards of ker-seymere
[cashmere] and eight yards of lining, all the same
color, to make me a dress. Everything matched.
We had hooks and eyes and all the trimmings:
ribbons, lace, and velvet binding for the bottom.

Dresses was a whole lot prettier then. Why,
I guess they were!

Why, I could take one yard of ribbon, tie it
around my waist, and make a double bow. You
see, we wore corsets with ribs that came up here in

the front and laced up in the back. They buttoned up, too, in the front.

I wore a twenty. How did they feel? They were just as smooth and tight as could be. Why, I just felt all right. My wedding dress was made just like the others. Every stitch I made by hand, and it was cream-colored ker-seymere and cream lace.

It had pink ribbon with pink velvet binding for the bottom. The basque [bodice] was fitted tight, and it had a five-gored skirt. I had a hat to match, a cream-colored panama with pink ribbon and pink flowers.

I got married at home, and we had dinner there. I don't remember what, just a regular dinner; then we left. But before I was married, my good old pappy bought me a cape—the prettiest cape around here. It was plush and worked all over in beads, with a fur collar. All black. Solid black. It cost $10.00 then. It would be a hundred now.

MINNIE LEE SPENCER, 1879
Stokes County

Gingham Aprons

Ginghams.
I had three or four little gingham aprons,
buttoned up the back.
And that's all I wore to school
was those little gingham aprons.
Washed 'em on the weekend.
And ironed 'em and hung 'em on the wall.
I'd wear one Monday and Tuesday,
then one Wednesday and Thursday,
and one Friday and Saturday.

Clothes hung on the wall.
There wasn't no such thing as closets.
Had nails in the walls.

And I was just crazy about those
little gingham aprons.
Oh yes, they had sleeves. Long sleeves.
They were open all the way
down the back with buttons on 'em.
And I just wore petticoats under them.
My mother would make me four.
Blue, pink, green, all different colors, you know.

And the dresses were down to the ankles then.
Little girls never wore anything except dresses
and aprons.
And long stockings. And bonnets.

MAGGIE JEFFERS, 1894
Cleveland County

The Cooler in the Well

And another thing
that most people did:

if you had anything
that you wanted to save,
you put it in a cooler
and tied a rope to it
and let it down
in the well, kind of,
to keep it.

The same well we got our water out of.

We didn't put it in the water,
but we dropped it down in the well
where it was cool.

I've dropped a many a bucket of,
cooler of something we wanted to keep—
buttermilk, sweet milk.

We didn't have no other way
of refrigerating it then.

HUBERT C. WOODALL, 1892
Johnston County

Making a Gum

Now, we had what we called a "gum."
There's a black gum tree. Well, it grows so much a
year, and there's a certain layer—why, you can
take the inner part out. You cut it down and let it
dry out, and then you take the inside out and leave
the outer part, and that is a "gum." That was set
up on a—well, Daddy would fix a little scaffold of
a thing—and he would set this up and Mother
would put rye straw down in the bottom of it, and
then she would pour ashes that she took out of the
fireplace where we burned oak wood or maybe
chestnut wood. So she would put that in this gum
and pour hot water over it. And that would drip
through, drip through, and that would make the
lye.

And then Mother would put that into a big kettle and boil it. And she would make liquid soap from it. 'Course, she'd put some other things in. And, if she wanted to, she'd boil it down and cut it out in pieces and have hard soap.

And that was good soap, but it was strong. Mother always kept other soap for us to bathe in.

NORA C. WAGONER, 1882
Alleghany County

Ash Hopper

They made the soap
out of wood ashes and meat skins.
And you've heard talk
about
your nose dripping like a ash hopper?

Well,
that's the way it dripped,
that ash hopper.

And they made soap out of it,
and that's the only soap you had
that would take the tobacco gum
out of your overalls.

But you didn't try
to keep your overalls clean.

When you'd go in at night,
you'd just stand 'em up in the corner.

The gum would hold 'em up straight.

LEE EDWIN KISER, D.C., 1898
Iredell County

Making Soap

In fact,
I remember
my Grandmother Phillips
was
making soap one day,
and
the pot was sitting
on three legs
on bricks.

The fire was under it,
and
she was stirring.

And it got off the brick,
turned over,
and
burned her ankle
very badly.

she had to use
a crutch
for a while,
it
was so hot.

LOUISE PHILLIPS KISER, 1898
Iredell County

Homemade Dyes

My mother
would take her some pokeberries
and make her some dye out of it
and dye her quilt linings with it.

And we dyed eggs with it, too.

We dyed with wheat.
Go to the field
and get green wheat
and boil it on the stove,
and you could make you a color,
kind of yellow.

And onion peelings made yellow beige, too.

Yes, it stayed in good.
Boiled it in.

And oak bark made a brownish color.

MAGGIE JEFFERS, 1894
Cleveland County

The Shuck Mop

And we made a shuck mop.
It was about that long
and it had holes in it,
and you stuck the shucks in there
and mopped and scrubbed the floor.

And Mama
would put sand down
on the floor
and scrub that sand
for her soap.

Or
sometimes
she'd put sand down
on the floor
and let it stay
a long time.

Everybody did.

MAGGIE JEFFERS, 1894
ETHEL LUTZ, 1898
Cleveland County

Flour-sack Towels

For towels,
we used flour sacks.

Very,
very nice.

They were very absorbent,
and to cut one half in two
made
two nice-sized tea towels.

And you could hem 'em.

They were very durable.

Made
nice dish towels.

Hand towels, as well.

LOUISE PHILLIPS KISER, 1898
Iredell County

Whitewashing the Fireplace

I want to tell you about—there used to be a lot of white mud. You'd go to certain banks; it was not just everywhere. In the summertime my mother—well, we had a big fireplace. I could stand up in it.

Well, my mother would wash and clean all the ashes out. She'd clean all that up good, get all the soot down and wash it real good with soapy water. And then she'd go to the bank and get white mud.

And she had a big old pot she made up the whitewash in, with cold water to mash it up good in, you know. And it would be just like paint. And she'd whitewash the fireplace all up good inside and outside. And it would dry.

And when that would dry, she'd go and get her some flowers or even honeysuckle or something and make her a big old flower pot and put it in there.

And the fireplace would be so pretty and smell so good.

BERTHA NORMAN, 1911
Burke County

Spring Housecleaning

There was a time when they felt that the old walnut pieces and the old solid oak pieces were, well, they were discarded or were put on the back porch or maybe put in the smokehouse just to use the new furniture. It was lighter weight and all that.

Of course, in the spring there was windows to be washed, curtains to be taken down, washed, starch 'em, iron 'em; and, 'course, they were washed with a little bit of bluing. Made 'em sparkle a little bit. White.

And the feather beds were sunned and aired and ready to put back on the beds for winter use. Of course, in the summer they were stored in the attic. People used straw ticks in the summer because they were cooler. Or later, there was the felt mattress. But the feather bed was put on for winter use because the feathers, you see, would tuck around you and keep you warm in winter.

As for the rugs, you'd put them out on the line and take a broom, a brushbroom, and beat 'em, knock 'em, dust 'em. And then, too, spring was a nice time to fix the slipcovers and freshen them up.

Then window-washing was usually a summer job. The rugs, mostly, were the home-woven rag rugs about a yard wide. And there would be strips of those put down. . . . They would be for winter use. Oftentimes, then, they'd put down the matting in the summer. It was cooler, and it was often changed for that reason.

LOUISE PHILLIPS KISER, 1898
Iredell County

Chinches and Flies

And the "tunnel bed," well, every day you'd make it up and push it under the big bed. And at night, why, Mother would tell us to go and pull our bed out. And we'd go to bed. Maybe two or three of us would sleep in that little bed.

Had a straw tick on it. Had straw ticks on all the beds. And Mother would take a time cleaning up.

And everybody in the country had chinches. And every—'bout twice a year—I'd just hate that so bad—'bout twice a year we had to carry everything out of the house, and Mother would fill our big old washpot full of water and get it hot and then she'd go in there and throw it all over the walls and scald all the walls down good. And it wasn't just us that did that; it was everybody.

Everybody had chinches. They look like a tick except they was bigger. Yes, they'd bite and suck the blood out of you just like ticks. Round. The hot water would kill 'em. For a little while. They were in cracks in the walls.

And we'd have to carry everything out and then carry everything back in, and that evening the house would smell so good. Oh, just so good.

No, we didn't have anything to spray with. There wasn't no such thing then.

And we emptied the bed ticks, every one of 'em. And we'd put fresh straw in 'em, and they'd be *that high* on the bed. And, oh, they'd just sleep so good. We'd crawl up on top of 'em.

And we always washed the bed ticks before we put the fresh straw back in 'em. That would be in the summer time when they'd thresh the wheat. Mother would say, "Let's go tell Daddy not to put all the straw up, to save some for the bed ticks."

MAGGIE JEFFERS, 1894
ETHEL LUTZ, 1898
Cleveland County

Homemade Flyswatters

And my daddy would take and make a flyswat out of the Sears-Roebuck catalogue. You know, a long handle. Mama would sew it, split the paper, or cut it with the scissors and tack it on that piece of wood. Whip it over and over, sew it along.

And Papa rigged up a paddle under the table. He sat at the head, and he put that stick on it, and it would go back and forwards to keep the flies off. If you didn't do that, somebody had to fan you.

I've seen folks go out and break off old brushes, break off a limb with the leaves on it. The flies were so bad. And there were no screens. Had to have the doors open.

And they'd buy a piece of net about this wide to go over the baby's bed because there were so many flies.

MAGGIE JEFFERS, 1894
ETHEL LUTZ, 1898
BERTHA NORMAN, 1911
Cleveland County

The Battling Block

Well, I guess you know about how we did our washing? We had a big block set up, and we had a big stick—a paddle. We called it a battling stick. And we had a large kettle where we heated the water. And Mother would heat the water, and we had wooden tubs. We didn't know what galvanized tubs were then. And Mother would wash the clothes, then put 'em in this big kettle and boil them. That was a big iron pot—a washpot. And they had white heavy goods then. Mother made all their shirts. And they were all white. We didn't have colored goods then, you know. And they had to be washed and brought out and boiled and battled and then washed again and then rinsed.

Yes, battled. We had this big block and a stick and we'd just come down on them and just *battle 'em*! And that beat the dirt loose. We'd take 'em out of the water and put 'em on the block, and they had plenty of water in 'em, and we'd stand back a ways and battle 'em.

And then we had a trough that the water run into from the spring. And it ran on into this box. And we put the clothes into the box of beautiful clear water and rinsed them and rinsed them. And Mother didn't ever have any wringers, you know. It was really too much for her to wring all those heavy clothes. We had so many. So we'd just hang 'em up and let the wind blow 'em dry. Just hung 'em up dripping wet.

We hung 'em on the fence. A paling fence was built. We didn't know what a clothesline was then. And they was hung on the fence to dry. And Mother usually made starch and starched some of the things she wanted to starch. We used to starch pillowcases and things like that.

How'd we make our starch? Well, we just had boiling water, and we took flour and stirred it up and made our own starch that way.

And then we heated our irons by the fireplace. Well, Mother would heat 'em on the stove sometimes, cookstove. We never had heaters, you know. We had fireplaces.

NORA C. WAGONER, 1882
Alleghany County

Cleaning Woolens

Now,
woolen things,
they were sunned and aired and brushed
and pressed.

And if they happened to get a spot on 'em,
we'd, of course, wipe it off with a damp cloth.

Wasn't such a thing
as dry cleaning then.

They didn't wash them until
they were quite aged.

LOUISE PHILLIPS KISER, 1898
Iredell County

A Cellar

There were some families
where I lived,
outside Morganton,
that had a cellar,
what they called a cellar.

And the ground
was real hard, red.
And my mother swept it
just like she swept her floors
and put her butter
in covered dishes
and her milk in crocks

and tied it up,
and it stayed just as firm.

And we had a door going
down in there
so nothing
could get down in there
to it,
you see.

BERTHA NORMAN, 1911
Burke County

Making Shoes

We had a man by the name of Elsdon who came to our house in the fall of the year. And he would measure our feet, and my daddy would buy the leather. No, he didn't bring it with him. We bought our own. And this man would come and stay with us and make our shoes. He would live in the house with us. It would take him about two weeks. You know, there were eleven of us. I've still got the lasts.

When they got the shoe shaped and were putting a sole on, they used wooden pegs. You can still see the holes on the lasts. When the shoe was finished, then they took it off the last and then they had an iron last that they put on and they put in the tacks. And the metal would bend them back. That was a finishing last.

Oh yes, our shoes lasted. They'd last a couple of winters. We didn't wear them in the summer, you know. We went barefooted in the summer.

No, he wasn't a bachelor. He had a family that he'd go back home to every once in a while. But he made shoes for all five boys in our family and us six girls.

NORA C. WAGONER, 1882
Alleghany County

Old Well Sweeps

On the farms, they had their old well sweeps,
and the depth would vary.
Some places it wouldn't be
more than eight or ten feet deep.
Other places, it was deeper.
I remember seeing the sweeps in the country.
It was not an uncommon thing.

A chain wasn't always available,
but this material was available.

A cypress pole wasn't difficult to come by.

I remember seeing some old wells
where they would use
the big old cypress hollow log,
I'm sure was what it was.
Now, I'm sure they either found it hollow
or they either hollowed them out,
because cypress was almost impervious
to weather,
and would last a long, long time.

LOUISE V. BOONE, 1922
Hertford County

The Cypress Stump

Well, it was a pole fastened to a fulcrum. The lower end of the pole rested on the ground, and it stood up at an angle over the well. At the upper end, they had a bucket fastened to a cord, or wire, or rope of some kind, or even sometimes, another pole.

And when the lower end of the pole was raised, the upper end sank down into the well. When you wanted water, you just let the pole down and you got your water.

Frequently, the well was covered with an old cypress stump. A hollowed-out cypress stump was placed over the well itself, so that the bucket went down into this stump, down into the water.

You see, here in Scotland County, the water is just under the surface. Because this is all sand land through here. This was seashore once upon a time. Before my day. And when you get up here in the upper end of the county, there are sand dunes. This we call the sandhills of the county.

And the water table here in this section of Scotland County is very close. You can drop a hollow pipe down about eight or ten feet, and you've got water. Good clear drinking water.

GERTRUDE M. KISER, 1897
Scotland County

A Place for the Well

I'll tell you, Mr. Welsh found the place
where I had my well
up here on the hill.

My well was out in the back,
and it was right down through—
it was solid iron ore.
When they got down there,
the water wasn't ever any good.

It was full of iron and it was bright red.

But they went down
a hundred and twenty-five feet to find it.

And he didn't use no peach-tree limb.

Come over there one morning and said,
"I'll find a place for your well."

And he did.
But it was an iron mine, anyway.

FRANCES C. COLE, 1890
Buncombe County

Thrift

But on the farm,
it wasn't so hard.
I didn't realize there was a depression.
Well, then you didn't demand
so much.
Never was there a time
when our family
couldn't get what they wanted.
We didn't ask for too much
because my daddy says,
''Don't ever want anything
you can't pay for.''

And my mother says she never
had to ask for a penny from my daddy
because she had her
chickens and her eggs.

And he'd take 'em into town
to Mr. Walter Welby's store
and bring her the money.
And until—but when Sister and Johnny
were off at school at the same time,
she just
had to ask for something
to get extra sheets with.

MARY C. MC KINNON, 1886
Scotland County

3   FOOD

Before the days of canning and freezing, kitchens of rural North Carolina were warm, savory places. Each meal was prepared from scratch, and pots bubbled over open coals or simmered for hours on the back of an old wood range. Hospitality was a sacred calling as neighbors and strangers alike were pressed to "Come on in for dinner" at noon. People ate what their land and their diligence produced. What they could not raise in their fields and gardens, they traded for. Waste was almost unknown as family members spoke for their favorite "parts" at slaughtering time. And the lowly ramp was sought in the land.

Water-ground Cornmeal

Well,
that
water-ground cornmeal

made
some of the best
hoecake corn bread

anybody
ever
put in his mouth.

I was brought up
on
hoecake corn bread.

Mother's corn bread
was better
than
some people's cake.

HUGH B. JOHNSTON, JR., 1913
Wilson County

All Kinds of Food

We had all kinds of food to cook, . . . but we didn't have glass jars to can in. I never saw a glass jar till I was about grown.

But we went out and put our turnips down and covered them up with straw, then covered that up with dirt and dug a trench around it and set up boards around it. And we had turnips all the winter that way.

And we had cabbage. We'd make up a bed just as long as a fence rail, and Bud would go to the field and get my cabbage plants where I had planted them and bring them back, and we'd set them plants down with their roots just that way, you know, in a row all across there, right close up. Then we'd put in another row and keep on till we had a square as big as the fence rail.

Then we'd build the rails up all around them just as high as the cabbage. And we'd lay corn stalks and pine limbs over the top to keep anything from bothering it. And we just had cabbage all the winter. They just stayed there and headed up the prettiest you ever saw.

And the same way with Irish potatoes. We fixed a kiln just like we did for turnips to keep our Irish potatoes in. And the same way for beets. We fixed a kiln. No, it wasn't a hole in the ground. We just built it up a little so no water would run in it and dug around it a little.

And they stayed just as nice and firm as could be. Whenever we wanted some, we just went right out there and got them.

And that cabbage bed would have sprouts on it, and we'd cook them just like cooking sallet.

Just as good as could be. And that's the way we fixed them.

And our cucumbers. We had a big barrel built, and we put them in it down in some salt and water, and they stayed just as good. In the winter time we'd take them in and soak them in clear water, then put them in salt water and vinegar. And they were just as good as could be.

The barrel set down at the spring on a big rock, and we could just wash the cucumbers and put them in and make a brine and that would keep them.

And we put apples in that barrel, too, and they would keep. The salt kept them from freezing, and we covered the top and tied a string around it.

And we made our preserves. And we had honey. My pappy kept bees. We had plenty to eat. My pappy never let us get out of something to eat.

MINNIE LEE SPENCER, 1879
Stokes County

Making Yeast and Bread page 33

And my mother
used to make her own yeast
to make her light bread with.
Made it out of Irish potatoes.
Scraped those Irish potatoes
and she had a little yeast left over
to start it off with.
And then put it where it was cool.
And it'd just be like yeast then.

And you could
smell
that
bread
cookin' for miles!

It'd smell so good.

Great big loaves!

Oh, it was delicious
when it was hot with butter.

BERTHA NORMAN, 1911
Burke County

Making Hominy

I've made hominy many times. Now, Grandmother Gardner put water on ashes, wood ashes. Or she'd take fresh ashes and put 'em in her pot that she was cooking and boiling corn in. The whole grains of corn. After it got hard. Hard corn. And you boil it until the peeling on the corn, the husk, it peels up. It will break right across the end . . . and peel up. And then you take your pot and run cold water in it, and it will all peel up all over it.

And they make the ashes out of hickory wood. They use hickory. And they can make the lye, but it's all made from ash to start with, just that old gray ashes.

And you wash it and wash it and wash it. We always had to take ours to the branch because you could never carry up that much water for it. Till all that old husk comes off. And it's pretty when you wash it. It comes out white, no matter what color the corn was.

And you cook it then for quite a while until it's tender. Just for hours and hours. Just in water. Plain water. It used to take Mother all day to make hominy. Hominy-making day was quite an event.

They used an old washpot. Great bit iron pot. And you'd make that about half full. Keep tasting it to see if it was done. We had that job. ''Go taste the hominy; see if it's done.'' And we just loved to go get out a half dozen grains and chew on it, you know. And it's good, too.

And then, later on, you cook your ham. And take out your hominy and heat that. Nothing better. Hominy and ham. Has a wonderful flavor for me. Hog and hominy.

FRANCES C. COLE, 1890
Buncombe County

Gathering Persimmons

My daddy used to dry persimmons.
He'd go and call us up every morning
before the frost got off of the trees
so they wouldn't mash.
And we'd go and get up in the trees,
some of us,
and pick two or three bushels
and put 'em in the wheat house,
we called it.
Put a sheet or something down,

spread it all down on the floor
and dry 'em.
And, oh,
they were the best things!
No, we didn't take the seed out.
Left it in there,
and they were so sweet and good.
We'd slip up there and—
my daddy kept it locked,
but if we could ever
get ahold of the key—
there was so many of us!

ETHEL LUTZ, 1898
Cleveland County

Spicewood Tea

Why, I used to dry
all kinds of food:
peaches, apples, blackberries, pears.

They gave me the name of the
best sweet 'tater pie in the country—
and the best apple pie—
and the best spicewood tea.

Down in the woods,
down yonder on that branch,
we could find the spicewood,
and I'd go down
and get those bushes
and bring them up here
and break them up.

Then I put them
in cold water with sugar
and brought them to a boil.

Best I ever drunk!

Wish I had some now,
but you can't hardly find
any spicewood now.

MINNIE LEE SPENCER, 1879
Stokes County

Leather Breeches Beans

Now, leather breeches beans
is a bean that's supposed to be
a tender bean.
People would make what they called
leather breeches beans.

What they did—they'd take and wash
their beans and break 'em.

Green beans.
Then, take you a needle and thread
and string 'em. Now dry 'em.

And in the winter, soak 'em and cook 'em
just like you would any bean.
They've got the best flavor you've ever seen.
Some people call 'em "shuck beans."

Now, to kill the germs or the bugs in 'em,
you just string 'em, then lay the whole string
in a pan and put it in the oven.

Then, just leave 'em there long enough
to kill the germs.

REED HAWKINS, 1895
Buncombe County

Molasses

And old fashioned molasses. Sorghum. We
had a mill that ground. You cut the cane and
stripped the fodder off. Cut the top off. It was just
in sticks. About six feet, some of 'em. And they'd
feed it into this mill, big end first, a stalk at a time.
Anyway, the mill just smashed it. Two big rollers
and one little roller. Ours was a three-roller mill.

Run that mill with a poor old mule or a poor
old horse. And he went around left-handed. A
pole leading him. A tether. And a funny thing, the
poor old horse didn't know he was leading
himself. But all the time he'd go around, that
would make the wheels in there turn and that
egged him on, you know. He had to follow this
stick that was fastened to him that was leading
him. And he was doing it himself, but he didn't
know it.

Somebody would put four poles down in
the ground and put leg bolts down on there. And
then John and Tom and maybe somebody else
could haul their cane in there and make it on
shares. They'd grind it, and then they'd have a big
galvanized tin pan there that Daddy made, the
molasses pan. And you boiled that juice. Just put
in the raw juice. Pan was eight feet long and about
that wide [measures] and that deep.

It would hold, I don't know how many
gallons it would boil down to, but it would be
filled almost full of the juice. But the faster they
would boil it, the brighter color it was. And if they

boiled it real slow and didn't take care of it, it'd get dark. Real dark. And, of course, nobody liked dark molasses.

Some people could make good molasses with the same pans, and others couldn't make it. And Papa said also that the soil that the cane was grown in, too, had something to do with it. The color of it. But each man would have five or ten gallons.

And they used to say when the cat fell in the molasses, they'd get him out and thrip him down—wait a minute—you haven't got the good part yet: they'd thrip him down, you know, so's not to waste it, and they'd say, "Give that to Mrs. Cowan." We'd get a share of it 'cause people used our molasses mill. We got a lot of it we couldn't use.

But Papa would go to pick up the toll. He'd say, "Now, whose is this? Speak up!"

And somebody would say, "That's mine. I made that."

"Well, now, you've got a bunch of children; you keep it." That's what he'd say if he thought the cat had been in it or something.

When they're boiling it, they stir it all the time, and somebody sets there and skims it. A froth would come up on top of it, and they'd take a skimmer they'd made on a long handle and skim it off. Then they'd take that skimming and pour it in a hole.

And, if you weren't careful, you'd be the one to step in that hole. We did. There was a whole bunch of us running through the meadow down there, going from the house to the spring. And they'd dug holes in the meadow and poured these skimmings down there. Don't know why they didn't pour it in the branch. The fish might have like it.

One day we were down in the meadow and were going to hunt guinea eggs. The guineas would lay a great pile of eggs. So we heard a guinea cackling, and we yelled, "Oh, a guinea's nest," so here we went. And two or three of us stepped in these molasses holes. One of 'em stepped in the hot. Most of it was cold, but this was the last they'd taken out and was hot.

D. C. COWAN, 1897
FRANCES C. COLE, 1890
Buncombe County

Ramps

Well,
ramps
is what I would call a
''I-don't-know-what.''

But it's the original;
it's just a *ramp*.

But I'd call him a cousin
to a onion.
But he grows wild.
He grows in rich coves.
Rich coves.
Mountain land where the coves is rich.
Rich, loose land.
And, instead of having a round blade,
he's got a flat blade.

But he'll make a little bitty head
like a onion.

He's got a onion flavor and
a loud odor to him.
Might loud.

And you'd eat him
just like you'd eat onion.

REED HAWKINS, 1895
Buncombe County

Walnuts

We used to have a few chestnut trees around.
But, by the time I came along,
the blight had just about killed all the chestnuts.

But we—Hermie, Hobert, Marvin, Edward,
and all the rest of us—
we sat over there under the walnut trees.

There was big old walnut trees just east
of my granddaddy's old house,
and we'd crack walnuts and eat 'em
for three or four hours.

They didn't seem to bother us.

If I'd eat a black walnut now, it'd kill me.
They were very rich.
We had an abundance of walnuts.

Those trees were planted
when my daddy was four years old.

About a hundred years ago.

LEE EDWIN KISER, D.C., 1898
Iredell County

Chestnuts

The chestnuts?
Oh, yes.
They were great big trees,
big body and long,
way up to the first limbs, you know.

And we'd just have chestnuts!
And there would come a wind
and you could just hear 'em a-raining down.
You could go out and pick up buckets full.

But the chestnut tree was, I expect,
four or five feet through.
The biggest one that I remember
was out at Mr. Cicero Boles's.

It stood out to itself.

And then they would split 'em and make rails, you know.
That was what they made the rail fences out of,
was chestnut trees.
It was a job to cut one down.
They had to chip 'em on one side and then saw 'em down.

But there come a blight and killed 'em all.

LELIA F. BAKER, 1903
Stokes County

Apple and Peach Trees

Down at my Grandfather Phillips's old home they had, when I could first remember, those large apple trees. There were three or four, oh, just tremendous trees. And there was a white apple that ripened right late in the summer. We called them "Aunt Sally." I don't know; I've never seen any anywhere else, but they were very, very nice apples for eating or for cooking. Aunt Sally apples.

My father said when he was coming up, just a boy, that at night they would peel apples. They had so many apples down there, and they would peel apples way into the night, till bedtime.

And they would dry apples. That was one way . . . see, there was so little money in the country then, and dried fruit was one way of having something to sell, you know.

And there were peach trees all over the plantation down there. My grandmother would plant, if she got a nice peach, one that was real nice, she would plant that seed in the stump of a tree that had rotted. She would put that seed in that rotting stump.

And it would be protected because when they would plow the field, they would go around the stump, you know, and the little old seedling would have a chance to get started. And when I could first remember, there were peach trees all over the place down there.

LOUISE PHILLIPS KISER, 1898
Speaking of her childhood in Stokes County

Apple Brandy

My granddaddy had all kinds of old—
well, they weren't particularly
outstanding apples,
but
some of them I remember were
the Merritts, which was a red striped apple;
the Buckinghams, which were green
with a few red stripes—
big, great big apples—
and then we had the yellow ones,
the Sugarballs;
and my dad had Rustycoats;
and, oh,
I don't know how many around there.

He distilled brandy,
but he did not make cereal liquor;
that is,
he didn't make whiskey out of corn or barley
or anything like that.

He just made apple brandy.

LEE EDWIN KISER, D.C., 1898
Iredell County

Hogkilling

Oh, Lordy, they used to build a rack. Put wood, just drive down four stobs and haul a big load of wood. And they'd put a layer of wood and a layer of flat rock, you know. And then put on more wood and another layer of rock.

And then you'd get up early and set that afire. About four o'clock in the morning. And that'd burn down, and them rock got hot, you know.

And they had a big hogshead. Buried one end in the ground. With water in it. And they'd take them rocks out on a shovel and put 'em in there. They'd just blubber and heat the water. And have an old quilt over the front end to keep the steam in. And that's the way they'd heat the water to kill the hogs before they had these vats. No, they didn't have the metal. These hogsheads were all wood. Big hogsheads, you know.

Just a few people had 'em. And they'd borrow 'em. Go way around, people in the neighborhood would have to wait till that fellow got through, or he'd take his hogs there and scald 'em. But they'd always have to make this—well, I always thought of when Abraham was going to kill Isaac, you know. But that's the way they'd do it. Just burned this wood with the flat rocks in it.

You couldn't put a flint rock in it because it'd burst. Had to have a sand rock. And when they put it in that cold water, that hot rock would sometimes shiver. Most of the time they just kept the rocks around close to the smokehouse where they killed hogs.

Oh, they'd start out about four o'clock in the morning. Cold? OOOOOOOOweeeee, yes, sir!

Well, they'd take till on after twelve o'clock, you know, to get 'em dressed and ready to cut up.

How'd they lift 'em? With man's strength! And they had a gambling [gambrel] stick. Folks used to have a stick to go between the hog's legs and it sharpened, and they'd cut these leaders in the legs here, you know. And hang 'em up. It would take two or three stout men to get 'em up there on the gambling place. They'd have a hole in the fork of a tree and a big stout pole crossed, and then they'd lift the hog up with the gambling stick between its legs and put the stick across that pole and hang him up.

And then they got to using single trees. But the old gambling stick—all that stuff—was put in the smokehouse and kept dry until the next hogkilling.

Yeah, they'd shoot 'em in the head. Or sometimes, they'd just stick 'em and let 'em walk till they bled to death. Just cut 'em right through the neck. They'd walk 'em sometimes from the pen—take an ear of corn and kind of guide 'em and walk 'em nearly to the scalding place and let 'em bleed good.

Then they'd cut their head off. Sometimes they'd be so big that they'd have to cut their head off before they took out the insides. And we were always there ready to get them brains when they cut that head open. We thought those were the finest things atall.

Lots of times they'd have 'em dressed till dinner, late dinner, you know; and we'd fry some of the liver, fresh meat. Always cut 'em up outside, the men did, and carried the meat all into the smokehouse.

My mama never would salt it down in the box till after night. She'd leave it laying out and let that animal heat get out of it, you know. And then she'd salt it away next morning. Unless it was freezing weather. Smokehouses, you know, was always dark and closed in pretty tight.

The meat boxes had to be plumb tight to keep the flies from getting in there. And they'd salt it down and leave it a couple of months in the salt. And then they'd take it out—the joints, all of it—and hang it up in the smokehouse.

Then they'd build a fire in, oh, a tin tub or a pan or something. Out of fire coals and get hickory—green hickory—and lay it on that and smoke this meat with green hickory and apple-tree limbs and a few sassafras limbs.

That would make the best-flavored meat you ever eat. Yes, the smoke just went up in the smokehouse. No, you didn't want no outlet. The smokehouse was tight, you know.

We'd all go and cut some hickory. You didn't want no blaze, just a smoldering fire.

And you had to be careful, too, about setting anything else on fire. Most of the time you'd take an old iron pot. And some smokehouses had dirt floors, and some, wood. But you'd set the iron pot up on rocks.

The last two or three days you'd smoke it—you'd smoke it about five or six days, you know—and the last two or three days is when you'd put these sassafras limbs and apple-tree limbs on it, and that would make it real good. Don't have no ham now like that. I smoked it as long as we had any.

LELIA F. BAKER, 1903
HUSIE ROBERTSON, 1906
Stokes County

Cooking Possum

Oh yes, the menfolks use possum dogs to hunt possum, and always at night. When the dogs tree it, they cut the tree down and put a stick in the possum's mouth. Then they pick it up by the tail and put it in a sack.

We still have a possum box. That's what we put it in while we fatten it. We fed ours on sweet potatoes, corn bread, and buttermilk for about a month.

When the time comes to kill it, we break its neck by hitting it in the back of the head with a stick. Some folks cut the head off, but others leave it on because they like the head. I never did. Then you scald it just like scalding a hog, and the hair will come off nice and easy. You can just pull it off or you can scrape it. Then you singe it like a chicken.

After that, you clean it and soak it overnight in salt water. Then the next morning, put it on to boil and boil it until about dinnertime.

During this time, too, you can be boiling sweet potatoes with the jackets on. When they're ready, you peel the potatoes and put them around the possum in the baking pan and put it in the oven. It will get so nice and brown, and then it'll be real good and tender.

My husband always liked to have possum for his birthday, along with chitlins. No, he didn't like either one of them, but he wanted them because that's what his mother always fixed for his birthday. Even though he didn't like them, the rest of us did.

RUBY B. KISER, 1912
Stokes County

Rabbit and Squirrel

We had squirrel and rabbit. We usually had those for breakfast. Oh, yes! That was good! Well, they set the rabbit gums to catch the rabbit. We never did have as many squirrels as we did rabbits. Papa and Worford and Forrest would set a batch of rabbit gums. They would have a regular route. Maybe they'd have a dozen gums, I don't know how many, but evidently they did.

And they'd go out early in the mornings, first thing. They'd go to the rabbit gums and get the old rabbits and bring 'em up, and they had a plank up there in the fork of a tree. Well, they put four nails up in there, and they'd hang that rabbit up by his hind feet and just skin it right down—it wasn't any trouble. Just split the skin on the back end and pull it right off.

'Course, Mama would clean it and salt it down, and we'd have it for breakfast. And that made the best gravy! The rabbit was good, but the gravy was better.

I guess the squirrel was about the same as rabbit. I didn't see much difference. Once I ate some hawk. Oh, that was the prettiest meat and the best-smelling meat frying you ever saw in your life! Just as pretty and white and tasty. It was as good as any young chicken. Emma fixed it [a neighbor]. Denver always did, every hawk he could get, he'd bring it home and she'd fix it. Just like a chicken. About like a pound-and-a-half fryer.

No, we never did have quail. Nobody in this family ever did believe in killing birds. As far back as I can remember, Papa never did ever let anybody bird hunt.

A lot of people eat frog legs. I know one night we stopped at Lola's, and she said, "Come here, I want to show you something," and Hollis had been out gigging for frogs. He had the prettiest bowlful of froglegs for her to fry. Now, those were pretty legs. They were almost as big as young chicken legs. People go frog-gigging up and down the creeks and around lakes and ponds.

Different people eat different things. Now, a lot of people eat groundhog. I know one man who bought a special gun to hunt them with. He just goes around and hunts groundhogs. He says it's the best meat he ever had.

Ted loved possum when he was a little boy. I've seen him stand up over there on that old bench beside Papa and eat possum and wipe his little hands on Papa's shirt and grin. And just eat possum like it was the best thing atall.

And another thing Mama would cook would be turtle. Got 'em out of that shell some way or 'nother. Looked like to me it was whole lot of hard work to get 'em out, but she'd get 'em out and fix 'em. Seems like to me she scalded 'em. But, you know something? They say that after you cook 'em and put 'em in the refrigerator, they'll come back raw.

But I do know that after they kill the things, for a long, long time they would still wiggle . . . quiver. I couldn't eat something like that. But Papa and Mama would eat it.

LUCY SPENCER, 1912
Stokes County

Dividing the Meat

I remember when a bear was killed, and the meat was used. It was divided up among the men that killed it. It was brought to my daddy's home. It was killed in Wilkes County near the Absher Post Office. It was a bear that had been in the Blue Ridge Mountains of North Carolina on the south side. And the men and their dogs ran it for days and finally it got down in the low country. And my daddy shot it. He killed the bear. Then a neighbor ran to it and stuck his knife in it and brought the blood, so he got the hide. The one who brought the blood got the hide.

And they got a team of horses and a sled and put the bear on it and drew it up the mountain to my daddy's to skin it. I was quite small, but I remember standing at the window watching out and seeing them skin the bear. A black bear. I was four or five years old. It was divided up among the men, but this Mr. Ellis got the hide. He had a coat made out of it.

Now, the meat was soaked in vinegar and salt to get the animal smell and heat out of it. And then it was soaked and washed and cooked. Oh yes, I ate bear, but I don't remember. I was quite small. To cook it they just boiled it in salt walter, I guess.

I do remember the oil that come out of the feet. My mother, she rendered the oil out of the feet. I don't know what it's there for, but it is. Well, she rendered it out and put it in a jug, and we used that for years. Bear's foot oil to grease our shoes with. We had cowhide shoes.

The bear-foot oil was nice for that. It kept our shoes polished up and kept the leather soft. And it waterproofed them, too.

NORA C. WAGONER, 1882
Alleghany County

Cooking Bear

Oh, yeah. We eat bear. Every once in a while. People do yet. Every once in a while we'll get a black bear in the mountains. Ain't you ever eat bear?

Well, the only way you go about killing it is just take you a gun and shoot it. But you first find it. And then, if you've got your gun and you can, you kill him. And when you kill him, you just hang him up and skin him and cut him up just like you do any other animal, a beef or hog. Just cut you off what you want, put it in a pot and cook it.

Skins easy. Skin comes off just about like you'd skin a calf or a cow. Naw, they're not hard to skin. I've skinned a many a bear. And a many a deer.

All we had in the mountains was the old black bear. You'd cook it just exactly like you'd cook a piece of pork or a roast beef. If you had you some good bear meat on the ham, or something, you'd cut you off some steaks and cook it just exactly like you would—takes you a little longer to cook 'em. It's a little tougher meat. No, no need to soak it.

It's an awful red meat. But a deer, he's more like a sheep. He's a light meat, a deer is. But a bear is a red meat. A bear tastes just like *bear*. It's a wild taste. Some wild taste. But it's good. It's good meat.

REED HAWKINS, 1895
Buncombe County

4 WORK

The North Carolina countryman lived by the creed of work. Many farm family days began before sunrise and ended after dark. Man had high regard for the work of his hands. His stature in the community was marked by the way he managed his crops and his property. In most instances the reward of hard work was simply pride in the accomplishment of a job well done. The whole family was involved, and young characters were frequently molded in the furrow behind the mule.

Work

'Course,
in those days,
work didn't mean much.

People didn't mind work.

They expected it.

They knew it.

And
they never
thought anything about it.

CHARLES L. REVELLE, SR., 1900
Hertford County

Teaching a Child to Work

If
you don't
teach a child
to work

before
he's seventeen,

he
never
will
work.

LEE EDWIN KISER, D.C., 1898
Iredell County

My Barefoot Tracks

I can remember well back around 1904 and '05. I was a little feller and I first remember helping my daddy plant cotton. I would carry buckets of seed to him to put in the planter. Oh, I was about six years old.

The next thing . . . I drug logs, took a mule or a horse to a log to drag off the ridges. All I had to do there was drive a mule. We laid off the rows, and there was a ridge about that high and sometimes it would be sort of sharp. Took a log and dragged over that and made a good seedbed for the cotton planter. The mule walked between two rows, drug two rows at a time. My barefoot tracks showed up behind me and that mule lots of times.

And later on, I got big enough then to hoe cotton. And then after I got big enough to plow, I began to plow a mule.

And, of course, it goes on up to laying-by time then. And that was a great time. Had a little vacation. Wade the branch. Build a pond on the branch. Have a big time for a while.

But then later on, when cotton-picking time come, then again, well, little fellers that high could pick cotton. They didn't have to bend their backs as much.

CARME ELAM, 1896
Cleveland County

Children's Chores

Now, children around the house were given things to do—pick up chips, carry out the ashes, bring in the water—some of 'em were taught to milk a cow, but I never got around to that. Cleaning lamp chimneys, Lord, yeah!

You ought to have heard Hermie one night. We come in down here, and Old Man Sutton, he was our teacher at school and also the Christian preacher up here. We didn't know he was in that front room down there asleep.

And Hermie took ahold of that lamp chimney, and it was still hot. And he had a choice exclamation, and Old Man Sutton just a-laying over there in the bed, our teacher and preacher!

He had a set of glasses that set on his nose like that, and one day he had 'em on his thumb,

and he was a-working so carefully among his
papers trying to find his glasses. And he had 'em
on his thumb all the time.
  Yeah, that hot chimney was pretty rough!

LEE EDWIN KISER, D.C., 1898
Iredell County, speaking of his boyhood in Stokes

Chopping Wood

Well,
we had to work like heck
in the wintertime
to get enough wood to run the fireplaces
so we wouldn't freeze to death.

And then we had wood choppings
  to get enough—
you know,
it takes several wagonloads to cure a barn of
  tobacco,
and we might cure
three or four or five barns of tobacco
in one barn.

And it took anywhere
from about five to eight acres on the farm,

cut each year,
of wood to run the tobacco barns.

You had
what they called wood choppings.

Folks got together and chopped wood,
and it was just the same way
with corn shuckings,
wheat threshings,
and all like that.

LEE EDWIN KISER, D.C., 1898
Iredell County

The Use of Animals

  Well, people just used oxen and mules and
horses and . . . just went out and tilled the land.
Man just used whatever he could get. A bull and a
bull-tongue plow and stuff like that.
  A bull-tongue plow is a plow where you
just hook one horse to it, and it's got a point on it
. . . we used to plow corn with 'em. Lay off corn
land with 'em. But you just make one furrow. And
it'll run from about four to five inches in width, the
plow point.

We made our own plows. Well, now'n, we'd
just take a piece of timber, about like a two-by-four,
or a two-by-six. You can hew it out . . . you can go
out there and cut you down a sapling and make
you a beam and then, of course, they had to go to
the shop to make a iron part.

But I've got one at the barn now that's all
wood. I'll take you and show it to you. It's all wood
except the point. The foot part, the part that goes
into the ground, is cut into the beam—what I call
the beam part; then it was pegged in there. And
everything is wood except the point.

We grew corn, tobacco, wheat, little buckwheat, potatoes and beans—just common rotation
of what people lives on.

REED HAWKINS, 1895
Buncombe County

Oxen

No,
it wasn't
that oxen were easier to work with.
They had the oxen
to haul

what a mule couldn't do.
They could get in rougher places than a mule.

We had two oxen,
Buck and Bealey.
They were steers.
Castrated bulls.

No, they're not like mules.
You know,
a mule can't have any little mules.
They're a cross between a horse and a jackass.

But an ox is just made from a bull.

And you know what?
You didn't have lines to 'em.
You just had a whip
and talked to 'em.

W. ROYCE MOORE, 1910
MINNIE E. MOORE, 1884
Forsyth County

NO HOLDINGS IN NWC - FOR HOLDINGS ENTER dh DEPRESS DISPLAY RECD SEND
OCLC: 2318393   Rec stat: c Entrd: 760609   Used: 900214
Type: a Bib lvl: m Govt pub: Lang: eng Source: Illus: a
Repr: Enc lvl: Conf pub: 0 Ctry: ncu Dat tp: s M/F/B: 00
Indx: 0 Mod rec: m Festschr: 0 Cont:
Desc: i Int lvl: Dates: 1977,
   1 010   76-20765//r85
   2 040   DLC |c DLC |d m.c.
   3 020   0807812889
   4 043   n-us-nc
   5 050 0   F259 |b .R68
   6 082   975.6
   7 090 |b
   8 049   NWCM
   9 245 00 Rough weather makes good timber : |b Carolinians recall / |c by
Patsy Moore Ginns ; J. L. Osborne, Jr., artist.
  10 260 0   Chapel Hill : |b University of North Carolina Press, |c c1977.
  11 300   xiv, 189 p. : |b ill. ; |c 17 x 24 cm.
  12 500   Edited transcripts of taperecorded interviews.
  13 651 0   North Carolina |x Social life and customs.
  14 650 0   Country life |z North Carolina.

  15 700 10 Ginns, Patsy Moore. |w cn
  16 700 10 Osborne, J. L. |q (Jesse Lee), |d 1923- |w cn

Cost of a Mule

And a good farmer, he'd brag about his animals. He'd take a pride in them. 'Cause . . . well, a mule cost a lot of money in those days. That is, according to the amount of money you had. A good mule was worth three hundred dollars way back yonder. And three hundred dollars was a lot of money back in those days. And they cared for 'em. Had to raise all the feed for 'em. You grew your corn. And in the fall of the year we used to, what we called pulling the fodder. We went by and stripped the stalks of all the blades and tied 'em up and tied 'em to the stalk. Or either we tied 'em up, and then somebody would come by behind you with a wagon and pick 'em up. And that's what they fed the horses and mules. Took it off the stalk and left the corn there. Left the corn there until later on.

Well, they did pull fodder, usually in August or September. It was a-turning brown. But then you had to go back and harvest the corn and then have what they called the corn shuckings. The neighbor would have his corn all piled, and they'd come and have corn shuckings. And the women would serve them meals, you know. Get together—family affairs. And not just families, but neighbors. And then, they'd do that same thing and go over to another neighbor's house. They did a lot of cooperative farming—not co-ops—but good old neighborhood farming. Good old neighborhood farming, just right.

HUBERT C. WOODALL, 1892
Johnston County

Clearing New Ground

My father and mother had only two acres of land cleared when they moved on the farm. And they owned close to two hundred acres of land.

He'd clear up a new ground every spring. And we children would have to help gather up all the stumps and roots and things, you know. Pile 'em up and burn 'em. And then a lot of times they'd just clear up the most beautiful forest you ever saw because they needed the land.

The stumps rotted out. And we dug 'em out by hand. And then some of 'em, they took and put a chain around 'em and let the mules pull 'em out. We burned 'em out, too. That was hard work. But it made wonderful corn. Just made the prettiest corn you ever saw. And took no fertilizer, just very little.

CLEO ELAM, 1902
Cleveland County

and distribute it along the rows.

Stink!
But it was dried.

MAGGIE JEFFERS, 1894
ETHEL LUTZ, 1898
Cleveland County

Natural Fertilizer

And we'd put out
for the corn,
my daddy
would haul a great big
load of manure in the wagon
and put it out
about middle ways of the field.

We had to rip open
the guano sack
and make us an apron,
and we had to put that manure out.

Fill our aprons with that manure
and take it

Lumbering

Early folks in these parts worked the log woods around here. They cut trees and used, oftentimes, oxen and mules in the early days to pull the logs up to where they could get 'em to load 'em on the wagons. Or get 'em down to the river to raft 'em, down the Chowan.

When they were moving the logs either up or down the river to the sawmills, they would raft them. In time past, there would have been three or four little sawmills at one place or another up and down the river. And if a man was selling, oh, say fifty, sixty, seventy acres of timber, whoever was cutting it, if he had to get it to the sawmill, oftentimes the easiest way to do it was to take those logs and just roll 'em down the hill to the river and line them up in a raft and float 'em to the sawmill.

Back then the rivers were the roads. It was the cheapest way to move anything. And logs would float.

It was common sense. And the people used their common sense. A great deal more than we do now sometimes.

Innate common sense and hard horse sense.

LOUISE V. BOONE, 1922
Hertford County

Using Skidpoles

My daddy
used to take the corner of a tobacco barn,
and
he knew how to notch those logs
just right.

And
they went up on skidpoles,
you know.

You pushed 'em up.
Yeah.
Just slipped 'em along the poles.

That's the way
you used to load logs
on a wagon.

LEE EDWIN KISER, D.C., 1898
Iredell County

Cattle Droving

Oh, law, yeah! I remember we always did drive the cattle. When I was a boy, we never trucked no cattle. I've drove many and many a bunch of cattle to Old Man Zimmerman's, down across this mountain. We'd just turn 'em loose. Gen'ally have us a good dog to hep us, and we'd just turn 'em loose in the road. Maybe ten or fifteen. And we'd just drive 'em.

Say you had a pretty good bunch of cattle and you wanted to sell fifteen or twenty head. You'd pick out what you wanted, fat enough, what you wanted to sell. So you'd pick up two or three men maybe, and say, "I want you to hep me go to market; I'm taking my cattle to the market."

And I've seen hogs go the same way. They'd drive hogs sometimes way down from Madison, part of Buncombe. Drive 'em to Asheville.

No, I know of 'em driving turkeys, but I never did drive turkeys. Well, they wouldn't fly away. No, a turkey don't, he can't fly much. He's too heavy. He can fly a little, or he can fly up on the roof. But, an old turkey, you can drive him just about as good as you can drive hogs or cattle. And they called that the drivers, or the drovers.

Now, as to how long it took, that depended on how far you lived from market. Say you lived—you could drive cattle somewhere in the neighborhood of twenty to twenty-five miles a day—but it depended on how far you lived. Say you lived forty miles from market, where you was going to dispose of whatever you had, if it was cattle or hogs. Well, it'd take you about two days. If you lived forty miles, it'd take you a day and a half or two days to get back.

Now, when nighttime come, if you had horses—which most of the time they did have horses enough to carry their men back—you could make it back home in a day, but if you didn't,

when night come, you'd try to find you a place like that down there, where there is a branch or spring. And you'd always take you some food with you. You'd take you a piece of meat; your wife or some of your folks would cook you a big piece of corn bread, and maybe you'd take a little coffee. So, when night come, you'd just park and feed your horses, cook you a little bite to eat, then lay down and go to sleep.

They'd gen'ally take some horse feed. Most people had saddle pockets on the horses when they's driving cattle or something like that, and they'd put 'em a little feed on their horse, or put 'em some in a sack or something, maybe in their saddle pockets. They'd gen'ally take a little feed to feed the horse. And then they'd let him pick, too, if'n it was in the summertime. But if it was late in the fall, maybe stuff all killed, he wouldn't get too much. He'd get a little dead grass and stuff, but he wouldn't get too much. You'd have to give him a little grain to help him along.

No, cattle don't stampede much. Not when man's handling 'em, driving 'em along. Oh, if you had a great big drove, they might. Say, you had a hundred and fifty or two hundred head. But just a few cattle's not apt to—oh, they might, now they might give you trouble. They're just animal. Usually, we didn't have too much trouble.

If you had a good dog, why he'd take charge pretty good. Well, we had mostly Red Devons. Just had different breeds of cattle, as fer as that's concerned. We had an old strain of cattle we called Old Brindle, striped mixture. We just called them Old Brindle cattle, but what they really was, after man come along and kept breeding cattle and studying cattle, was Guernseys. Actually, they was Guernseys, after they kept breedin' 'em up.

They had a stripe dark, and then light— they was ugly things.

REED HAWKINS, 1895
Buncombe County

Prospecting

They told me
them iron mines
was just somebody's gimmick
of gettin' something to eat.

Old Man Yancy,
all summer he come here,
and he'd stay a month with you

and dig
and have you a-thinkin'
he was going to find everything—
iron, gold—
and then he'd go up to Mr. Cowan's house
or Mr. Walter's or somebody else's.

And them places
was just full of holes
all around there.

They just fed him.

They didn't pay him.

He was just prospectin',
tryin' to find something for you.

REED HAWKINS, 1895
D. C. COWAN, 1897
FRANCES C. COLE, 1890
Buncombe County

Panning Gold

Yeah,
they found a
little gold in some streams.

They'd panel out a little.
Panel out a little gold.

One old man told me they found
a little gold down here
in this creek below the house.

REED HAWKINS, 1895
Buncombe County

Dip up a little
sand and water
and swish it around that way,
And the water,
you know,
would go out.
And, finally,
you know your gold is heavy.

It stays in there.

D. C. COWAN, 1897
Buncombe County

Moneysite

My daddy built a big two-story house, and the moneysite [monazite]—now, that's what they called it back then—moneysite, came in, and they'd sell moneysite. They'd work it out in the branch. They had a big old trough. And our two brothers, they'd shovel up that sand in the big old trough and get the moneysite out of it. It was high back then. You just got a lot of money.

My daddy tried his best—he had people down there digging for that mica, but he never did find that. But that moneysite, just everybody got rich off of that.

They had a big old trough, and then they had a iron thing put up here with little holes in it, and they'd throw the dirt up on that and the moneysite would go down through them little holes. Then the water would wash all the sand out. And it would just be black and with a little gold all through it.

And it would be so heavy you could hardly lift it. I couldn't tell you what they used it for. We sold it and made enough to build our house. Two-story house.

MAGGIE JEFFERS, 1894
ETHEL LUTZ, 1898
Cleveland County

Digging Wells

Well, man would just take him a shovel and just cut him a hole, oh about four or five feet—a circle—and he'd just keep goin' on down. And go right on till he hit a vein of water. That's all. He just done it by hand.

There's some people, now, Old Man Harry Lovell, he said he could tell you where water was. He'd get him a peach-tree limb, you know, and walk around, and he said the closest water vein, why, it'd tell. I never did put much faith in that, myself.

But that's the only way. They just used shovels and picks and mattocks. Just dug a hole and kept goin' down.

They put on a windlass. Now, what I'm a-talkin' about, a windlass, you took a—just like a big pole and a big rope—and you set your pieces out here to hold that pole up and then you put you on a bucket and let your bucket go down. And the man working in the well, he'd fill that bucket full of dirt and two men on top would roll it out and one would hold it and the other would take the dirt off, empty it, and send the bucket back down.

Sometimes they'd go down eighty or ninety feet. Sometimes a hundred, right down in the earth. Now, if they hit rock, the only way to get through it was to take you a piece of steel, drill it, put you in some dynamite, and blast it.

And you didn't know whether that man up top was goin' to roll you up fast enough or not! That's right! Had to use a pretty long fuse. That's the only way you had.

REED HAWKINS, 1895
Buncombe County

The Blacksmiths

Now, these old smiths,
they done it by hand.

It was man's work by hand.

He didn't have any fine tools.
And he didn't have any welding torch.
It was all just done by good common sense.

Just like I said about digging the well:
it's man's skill and ability to do
like—old people used to make their nails.

They just got metal and het it
and just cut it in pieces and made nails.
Made cut nails.
Square.
One end smaller, so it would penetrate,
so you could take a hammer and drive it.

REED HAWKINS, 1895
Buncombe County

Making Wagon Tires

Well, now'n, a man would just have him a shop. Shoe horses. Put on wagon tires. Make upset axes. And done just iron work, mostly iron work. Shoe oxens.

Now'n, they'd put on—in other words, you needed a tire on your wagon wheel or on your buggy wheel. Well, they had to buy the iron.

And the iron come in lengths. Different lengths. Well, the smith, he had to measure your wheel. Roll it out.

Then he'd measure his iron. And he'd cut his iron and then he'd bend it and weld it together. Now, to bend it, he het it. He put it under heat and bent it. You know, you can heat iron and bend it any way you want to. So he het it.

Then, when he got that, while it was hot, he had to cool it right quick 'cause it would burn the wood. But it would set in the wood some. So he put that on a stand that he had, and he'd take that band, which was the tire, and he'd take and put it on there and hammer it down.

Then he had a can of water there. Half a barrel of water, and he'd just take and roll it through the can of water. And that cooled it, you see. Psssssstttt! And it would draw up tight.

REED HAWKINS, 1895
D. C. COWAN, 1897
Buncombe County

Going to the Mill

When I was a kid, Saturday was the time most folks would take off from work. Sometimes they would work until noon on Saturday, depending on how pressing things were on the farm. But if things were not really pressing, they would go into town on a buggy or a wagon before the days of the automobile, get whatever supplies they needed and bring them out.

People grew the majority of their food on the farm in those days, and when they wanted cornmeal, people like my grandfather and other folks around would just simply take two or three sacks of corn down to the mill and get it ground and bring it home and put it in the pantry and hope that the weevils wouldn't get into it too badly before time to grind some more.

HUGH B. JOHNSTON, JR., 1913
Wilson County

Grinding Corn

Now, there were two types of stones they had around the farm. One was the actual grindstone which was fitted in a frame and had a crank so that you could crank it and turn the grindstone that would revolve, and you'd just hold your axe or blade just that way [demonstrates] to it.

And some would rig up some sort of a treadle, and they could work it with their foot, sort of like an old spinning wheel. Grandfather had one down by the old barn. The barn's still there, but I don't know what became of the old grindstone.

But I have several of those old millrocks out in the yard. Those old hand-mill rocks. You see, those big rocks they had in the mills, powered by water, were huge things. Now, these handstones were usually about two feet in diameter, and they were fixed up in a frame with the upper stone on an axle, and there was a handle. And so you fed the grain in there between the upper and another stone, and you could grind grist, which was a rough-ground corn. And you could make hominy grits out of that. Or you could feed it to your chickens. Little chickens—biddies.

Osborne

And all the rural families of any means at all had at least one of those hand-mills around during Civil War days, and they could grind rough corn. They couldn't make meal, I guess. But at least they could grind the grains up with those stones small enough to make hominy grits or chicken feed.

HUGH B. JOHNSTON, JR., 1913
Wilson County

No Vacation

We did not make trips away. We didn't have the money for it, and we didn't ever think about it. As for a vacation, we didn't know anything about a vacation. The big time would be in the fall. Most of them would take a day in the fall and a day in the spring and go into town, the ladies. In the fall, they'd go and buy what they needed for the winter. In the spring, they'd buy for the summer.

Now, they would use some money for that. That was after they sold their crop, what they had. Had a few peanuts to sell, and cotton was a big item here in this part of the country at that time. Cotton was referred to as "King." And we grew a lot more cotton than we did peanuts. And we'd pick that cotton and sell it. And that would take care of the cash needs, that and the few peanuts we sold.

We didn't sell livestock in those days. Very little. We would grow the hogs that we'd need and butcher them. We'd salt it down and hang it up. We'd kill one in the fall in order to carry longer by hanging it when it was cold.

We had no refrigeration back then. I've heard of ice being cut and stored back then, but we never did it. I remember we had some awful cold weather way back then. I remember very well in the teens, '17 and '18, the rivers froze over.

We grew other crops. We didn't grow too much tobacco. In the early days, Murfreesboro had the advantage of having a river. The Chowan. We shipped everything by boat.

In fact, this was a port for the country on up as far as Durham. Because back there, there was no railroad. That was in the early years. And the boats, they were running here and very active, up into the early teens.

CHARLES L. REVELLE, SR., 1900
Hertford County

Hauling Fishheads

I remember hearing
people around home
talk about taking their cart and going,
when the fishery was in operation,
and getting these heads;
and what they do,
they just take the fish
and cut his head off
and just slit him right down to the bottom,
that's it,
just pull the insides out.

And people would take that
and spread it on their fields.
And then
I remember hearing
some of the old women say
they couldn't stand to go outside the house,
and they'd have to pull the windows down.

That was their fertilizer.

LOUISE V. BOONE, 1922
Hertford County

The Great Catch

The men
just stood in their boots
and some
in their bare knees or breeches legs
with these herring
just jumping
and floundering—
it looked like silver
jumping all around them.
Live fish up to their waists.

I remember seeing that
as a child,
seeing those great catches come in.

And
they would have
to pull in part
of the net at a time
because
it would be so heavy with fish.

LOUISE V. BOONE, 1922
Hertford County

Moonshining

Well,
people used to,
they'd make 'em a little whiskey.
They'd get 'em up a little still,
and they'd get 'em up a little cornmeal,
and they'd sour it up, run it through the still,
and make 'em a little whiskey.
And they might let their neighbor have a little of it.
And they'd use it for theirselves.
They'd drank a little of it theirselves.
And they might sell a little of it.
See?
Now, what I mean by blockade liquor is this:
the man who was makin' blockade liquor, uh,
the government didn't get no revenue off of it.
And they called it "blockade" because
the government didn't get no revenue off of it
        atall.
Now, you go down yonder to that liquor store,
and you buy some liquor.
Well, the taxes was paid on that liquor,
and, of course, it's charged in the price of the
        liquor.
So you're paying a tax on that liquor.

Ain't no way you can get it without it.
Unless you make it.
You can make your liquor and the government
        don't know
nothing about it.

REED HAWKINS, 1895
Buncombe County

Government Stills

Now, back when I was a boy, I knowed of two government stills.

Old Man Boaz Riley had one. And he lived right at the edge of Madison County. Old Man Jess Pitt had one, and he lived on up on Turtle Creek.

Government still—you had to have a revenue man there. A storekeeper and gauger, they called 'em. And your government still—you're running a government still. All right, the government would hire *me* to stamp that liquor. Well, what liquor you run off, whether you run off two barrels or four barrels, the government got a dollar and ten cents a gallon back when I was a young'un.

Now, back then, if you could get it, you could buy blockade liquor for eighty or ninety cents a gallon, but the revenue on it cost you more than the liquor cost you.

Now, if you had a government still, the government would hire a man to check your still, and all the liquor you made, you had to put a government stamp on it, just like you stamped a letter. And that went to the government, and you had to pay that just like a sales tax or anything else.

Now, what I was going to tell you: these men would, if they could catch the man gone—or if they could do anything about it—they's just trying to make a living, and they wanted a little extra money. If I could get you off to town—if you was checking my outfit—and I could get you to go somewhere, or if I could get your back turned, and I could run a barrel of whiskey and roll it and get it out of the way, I could sell that whiskey and get by without paying any taxes. That's right.

Now, there was this feller by the name of Wes Dudley; he drove an old pair of mules for Old Man Boaz Riley, and he said about once every two weeks, Old Man Riley would try to get as much as two barrels, which would be about 110 gallons of whiskey. He'd try to get that out of the way . . . and he sold it to Dab Gilley or Seth Johnson for a dollar a gallon.

Now, the government stamp on that would be a dollar and ten cents a gallon, but I could sell it to you for a dollar because I didn't pay no tax on it. It was my liquor, all right; I made it. It was mine, but I didn't pay no tax, so they called it, you know, your bootlegging liquor. You was a bootlegger.

Made it out of corn. That's right, made it out of corn. Oh, yeah. They made rye liquor, too. Made rye liquor.

REED HAWKINS, 1895
Buncombe County

The Sheriff's Account

I cut up 147 stills in four years. I was figurin' I was gonna get 50 a year, but I fell short a little. As time went on, you know, I cut up so many, it put a lot of 'em out of business. The first year I got fifty, and the last year I only got twenty-five. A lot of 'em went to the road. I arrested, and there was eighty convicted the four years I was in office for making liquor and selling it.

A lot of 'em took pride in their work. In fact, it kindly runs in the family. I've even seen fathers take little kids five and six years old with 'em to the still. And they just growed up in it; they didn't think there was anything wrong with it. That was their family business.

In fact, way back in the mountains, they practically had no other way to live except to make a little liquor like that, you see, and sell it. You'd be surprised how some of 'em lived way back in the mountains. You couldn't hardly find room enough to make a garden, it was so rough. You can see why—it'd just run in the family for years and years.

Well, as a rule, they would have six or eight, what they called ''beer boxes.'' Big beer boxes, hold anywhere from a hundred gallons on up. Then they had a big boiler that they'd put this mash in, you know, and cook it. Then it went from that through a copper pipe into a still. Now, that's where, when this beer is cooked, it goes out as a steam, but when it goes through this still, it's condensed and comes out as a liquid. Distilled. You've got to be on a stream. The colder the water, the better it is. The better it condenses—the quicker, you see.

Well, they usually try to get into a thicket, like a laurel thicket or something. And I've known them to be two miles—you'd have to walk that far to get in there. Pack all the grains and chop and stuff in and carry the liquor out. And rough, too. Why, a lot of places it was a real job just gettin' in and out.

One place in particular down here, there was a rock, a big flat rock that crossed the road there. Just a solid rock, and it run way out in the woods there. Well, these bootleggers, they'd pull out on this rock there and unload their feed and walk way out on this rock.

Usually, when you're checking, you'll check fairly close to the road for a path leading out. And they would use this rock to go way out there on, and then at the end of this rock was a slick path. They used every means . . . why, they just tried to outsmart the officers.

I've had the branches shot off from over me. Oh, yes. On two or three different occasions. Just trying to scare me, I'm sure. I got a lot of threats, but I never was injured or anything.

Well, I had the confidence of the people. You know, my father had been sheriff. My father was sheriff in 1910 to 1914. And then I went on in 1946. Only time in Alleghany County that there was a father and son both sheriff.

Oh, we caught a good many. Lots of times we'd locate a still and if they weren't there, we'd check it then every night for so long.

They usually made it at night. Yes, they'd have a fire and a smoke, but it was so far back that it was hard to locate them. I have located a few off the Blue Ridge Parkway with some field glasses,

way back over the side of the mountain.

Sugar? You'd be surprised. You remember when sugar was rationed, the bootlegger, he could get sugar paying forty dollars a bag. And a bag of sugar would make ten gallons of liquor, see? He had sources, just put up the price, and he'd get most anything at any time, you see?

And we had a merchant here in town. I don't know what connection he had, but he furnished several bootleggers. I believe the most sugar I ever captured at a still was ten bags—a thousand pounds.

Very little of this was corn liquor. Most of it was made out of wheat chop and stuff like that. That was just plain old—now, if you made it out of corn, you called that "corn liquor"—but this other was just plain old, they called it mostly "bootleg." It was cheap to make.

They usually put it in jars, mostly fruit jars. Half gallons. And a lot of them would put it in these five-gallon cans.

I think a lot of it went into West Virginia. It was transported there. A lot of it came right through town here [Sparta], you see. But you'd never know who was doing it.

Here and in Wilkes County, you know. Wilkes was the headquarters for it. It used to go by the name of the "Bootleg Capital." They used to come here in pickups and cars. Why, you could haul fifty to one hundred gallons in a car. I've seen where it was just packed full, the trunk and the back seat. Usually the bootlegger would run it himself, or someone would come up, he'd sell it to 'em, up here. Then they'd take the risk.

There used to be a feller back out here who was in the liquor business heavy. He sold it, had it made and sold it, and he was living back out here in the mountain. There was a main road that went by his house and went on around and down. But from his house, there was kind of an old sawmill road that he could cut off there, and those fellows would come up there from maybe Greensboro or Winston-Salem and buy twenty-five or fifty gallons, you know.

And he got hold of a patrolman's uniform, a regular patrolman's uniform. Well, the minute they left, he'd jump into that uniform and get in this Model A Ford and cut 'em off down there, see? They'd be on the road, and, of course, he'd stop 'em, you know, and . . .

"Boys, I'm sorry, but I'm gonna have to see what you're hauling." And these fellers he'd just sold it to, but he'd changed his clothes so they wouldn't recognize him. Said, "You seem like pretty nice fellers. I hate like the dickens to take

you in. I believe I'll just confiscate your liquor and let you go on." So he'd load that liquor into his car and . . . resale the same load. Now, that actually happened.

And that's the way he got caught. He got eight years in the penitentiary.

But he had a good business going there for a while.

I don't think I ever found over two or three radiators with all the stills I ever cut up.

Now, there were three or four cases where the women were just working right with their men.

We had one feller here. He used to make liquor for, what you might say, all the big shots. Like anyone around the courthouse that drank. He'd make it, and they'd usually get five or ten gallons in their keg. And he was just as particular in making that liquor as you would be in your kitchen.

When he'd run off a batch, he'd take those barrels or boxes and clean 'em out, sweep 'em out, scald 'em out, and they were just as clean. Then he'd start all over again. And he used to sell to, I guess, a dozen men around here. He made mostly just about what they wanted. I guess he made mostly corn. And peach brandy. Sounds good? Smells good, too.

Now, I've had people come to me and want to know how much it would cost them for me just to leave 'em alone, lay off of 'em, not bother 'em atall. But I never got a report on a still that I didn't check.

No, I've not always taken men in with me. I've cut up several myself. I caught two men one time by myself. No, they never tried to offer any resistance when I caught 'em, except they'd try to outrun me, try to get away. And most of the time I'd have to get hold of 'em.

I knew practically everybody, and I very seldom ever brought a man in. If I knew him, I'd say, "Now, you come on up to the office in the morning and fill a little bond." Never had but one feller refuse to come.

They'd just come on in on their honor. I had one boy I forgot when I caught him that I'd had him up before and he'd got a suspended sentence. Sentenced him for twelve months and suspended it on the condition that he didn't make any more liquor or fool with it. Well, I caught him a short time after this. I didn't think about it, and I said, when I got ready to leave—there were two of 'em—said, "Well, you boys come on up in the morning and fill a little bond."

They said, "Be right there, sheriff." So, the next morning about nine o'clock one of 'em came in.

I knew they lived right close together. I said, "Where's Barney?"

Said, "Well, I come by his house, but there wasn't nobody there." And it just dawned on me then that he was under a suspended sentence. So I went right out there, and a neighbor said he'd loaded up last night and left about ten o'clock.

You know, that boy went to Maine, married and went up there, went to work, and they tell me he's got a beautiful home and family and doing fine. His father-in-law told me—I knew him well—he said that was the best thing that ever happened to Barney. But if he'd went ahead and served his sentence, he'd got out and gone right back into the moonshine business again. But we kept it on our docket here for about three or four years. We'd call him out every time, just finally dropped it.

A lot of 'em was just as law-abiding as you or me, except for that liquor business.

I've had 'em say to me, "Now, I don't steal, and I figure a-makin' this liquor, we work for our money."

GLENN D. RICHARDSON, 1897
Former Sheriff, Alleghany County

5   CASH CROPS

Cash income crops in the state were few, the main ones being tobacco and cotton. During harvest season conversation centered mainly around markets, warehouses, pounds, and prices. Although the process of producing a crop was honed to a fine art, eventual success still depended on the whim of the elements. Rain, sun, storms, and hail could make or break a profitable season. However, the North Carolina farmer lived as much on faith as profit, and he would soon be about his plans for the next year's crop.

Tobacco Gum

Now,
the gum would stick to your hands
so much,
though,
that you'd tear the leaf with it.

So,
to keep from doing that,
you had to reach down
and
get some dirt
and
put on your hands.

And
you'd better take you a match
and
singe all this hair on your wrists off
because
the gum would get on there
and
pull it terrible.

LEE EDWIN KISER, D.C., 1898
Iredell County

Cutting the Stalk

Back when I was a boy, they made barn-cured tobacco, and there wasn't any warehouse anywhere around Asheville then so we had to ship our tobacco to Tennessee or Virginia. We shipped it on trains, and we packed it in hogsheads. We

made them out of wood. We just went out there and cut down some white oak.

You cut that tobacco and put it on sticks and hung it up in the barn. Cut the whole stalk. Then you cured it, and what I mean by curing it was, when they built them barns, they build 'em with a furnace all the way around. Out of rock and mud. Start here at the front of your barn, and they'd build an opening to where you could fire it. Then they went all around the barn with flue lines.

Then you fired it and got your temperature up to where you wanted it, and you tried to hold it there for about thirty-six to forty-eight hours. Then you could go to slacking off because your tobacco would be pretty well cured.

Then when it was cured, you worked it off. You pulled off the leaves and tied 'em up in a little hand and packed it wherever you was going to put it till you got ready to put it in a hogshead.

Now, you can't work it till it's in case. The weather. But, if you wanted to, if your barn was cured good and you wanted to work it off fast, you wouldn't have to wait. You could put you some water in there in barrels or tubs and steam it, and you could bring it in case. It'd be like a lady ironing her clothes. You don't want to iron a piece of clothes unless you've got a little moisture on it to where your iron will iron it smooth and pretty.

Well, now, the only way you had to go to market was to put the hogsheads on a wagon and take 'em to a depot, wherever it might be, and ship it to Danville or anywhere that you had a market for tobacco. Lynchburg, Danville, and there was a place or two in Tennessee.

REED HAWKINS, 1895
Buncombe County

To Market on Wagons

Law me! When they used to take the tobacco, it'd take 'em three or four days to get to Winston and back. Because the mud was hub-deep sometimes. And the stock would give out.

And there was a certain rest place over there near where Boyles's store was, right over there near Mount Olive. They'd stop there and feed the horses, and they had a camp ground there. And they'd camp. Spend the night. And go on to Rural Hall and spend the night again. And then go on the rest of the way.

And that would be starting from around Moore's Springs.

MINNIE E. MOORE, 1884
Forsyth County

Barrels Drawn by Oxen

I heard how Lynchburg Road got its name. Well, way back before they had wagons, even, they'd put tobacco in big barrels and that pin that went through 'em was a lynch pin, they called it.

And they pulled 'em with oxen, just a big barrel. Rolled 'em. And that's where they got the name because on that road was where the man lived that started that thing. He's the first one who built a lynch pin.

All the way to Winston. Some of 'em rolled it as far as South Carolina. See, then they had bootleg tobacco in South Carolina.

W. ROYCE MOORE, 1910
Forsyth County

Flue-cured Tobacco

We just worked eighteen hours a day priming and hauling the tobacco in and tying it and putting it on the tierpoles. And the other six hours while we were resting, we'd fire the flues of two or three tobacco barns with heavy cordwood. That was the six hours while we were resting.

Now, the idea about curing tobacco is a matter of the control of air. While it is yellowing, you don't want any air on it. You want moisture, sort of a 90 or 95 degree temperature. And if you don't have enough moisture in the tobacco, you put some water in the bottom of the barn.

When it gets as yellow as you want it, then you raise your heat to maybe 180 degrees and kill out the stems. You raise it gradually from 95 up to around 120 and 130, and you open up the cone of the building—the highest point—to let this heat come out and bring it through the tobacco, you see? Let it in through the bottom and through the tobacco so it can dry it at that yellow stage in which you've got it. But you don't yellow it thataway.

About three days, something like that, to cure out a barn of tobacco. But we had to stay awake, you see, to do it. If you let your heat drop after you cured your leaf, well, the juice from the stem would run out your leaf and ruin it. It would splotch. They wouldn't give you anything for it.

'Course, we had it on the stalk a while there, like they do the burley tobacco now. Split the stalks, cut it off at the bottom, and hang it on the sticks. Whole tobacco stalk. Whole plant. The top was real green. And the bottom, it had holes in it, lugs. And in the middle you got your nicest leaves.

LEE EDWIN KISER, D.C., 1898
Iredell County

Sleeping at the Barn

Now, down here was a big tobacco town. Smithfield. And we'd have to go through the fields and pull off the lower leaves and then cure them—put 'em in a barn. You pulled 'em off and put 'em in what they called a drag truck that dragged it down the line and then they pulled it to the barn and they'd tie it, put it on about a four-foot stick. And then they hung it in a barn. The tiers in the barn, oh, I guess about fifteen, twenty feet high. Then you cured it. Oh, the pipes went all the way around, big pipes, about a foot through.

And then somebody had to stay up all night with it and keep that fire at an even temperature. Barns made out of logs and they'd take and daub it with what they called daubing, made out of a little cement. Put one log right on top of the other 'un. You see right many of those right on now.

Then you had to cut your wood in the wintertime for your tobacco barns. Pine or any kind they had on the place. Oak wood was mighty good.

But, as I said, somebody had to sleep at the barn. Had an alarm clock to wake him up at a certain time to check the heat. It was awful important that you kept that heat at a certain temperature. If it went up and down, you didn't get a good curing of tobacco.

Here we had a market in Smithfield. One of the first markets ever in this part of the country around here. Before, I've heard talk of when they used to have to take and put it on the train here in tow bags, tie it up, and carry it to Wilson to sell it. Then they didn't have a market here. But we've had a market here since I've ever known anything about tobacco.

HUBERT C. WOODALL, 1892
Johnston County

Cotton and Tobacco in Johnston County

Down here, we led the state in cotton and tobacco for a number of years. 'Course, not much cotton is grown anymore. It's been a fairly good county all the time, and we've never had much poverty. And everything was done by mule and a plow in those days. And a farmer, if he was a good farmer, would have four or five mules and a couple of horses. The horses were used—buggy horses—to pull a buggy to get to town.

And you got up about four o'clock in the morning. And you went to the field. And you had to break your land with just a little plow and a mule. Maybe they'd have two or three doing it. But about an acre or two was about all you could do in a day. One row at a time. Then, after you broke that land, you had to go back and run the rows for cotton. Run them for corn. Run them for tobacco.

If it was hard land, you used a disc [harrow] that was pulled by mules or horses. It took several times to ever get your land to where you could tend it.

When we were children, we had a farm out here, and we'd go out in the summertime and work, summertime, help pick cotton, hoe corn. The corn, they used to plant it pretty close together. Then they'd go through and chop out a whole lot except the ones they wanted to grow. Like they did cotton. The same way.

Cotton was sowed solidly. Then you had to go back—the women did most of the chopping of cotton—and farming was rather hard work in those days. You had to walk every step of the way.

HUBERT C. WOODALL, 1892
Johnston County

Fertilizing Cotton

And when we were planting the cotton or the corn, mostly the cotton, we had a big long horn and you'd walk along and take your hand and you had a big sack of fertilizer around your waist here. And you'd reach in there and get it and walk and put the fertilizer out, you know, along, through that horn.

That horn went plumb to the ground. It was about a yard long. And it was made out of tin and had a funnel on it. We used that to keep the wind from blowing all the fertilizer away.

We'd just stick our hand down in that bag and put it in the horn and just go along, just as far as that would go. Then we'd have to go get some more fertilizer.

Just keep a-walking, fertilizing that cotton. And the cotton would come up thick, and we'd thin it out, 'bout a foot apart. And we'd keep hoeing the grass out of it till it got up so big. And when it got up so high, we'd lay it by.

And then the bloom would come, then the boll, then the cotton. Then we'd go to picking. Pick in big old sheets and sacks.

MAGGIE JEFFERS, 1894
ETHEL LUTZ, 1898
Cleveland County

Growing Cotton in Scotland County

Every farm had a lot of tenant houses. Each one would have a family in it, and the man of the house would make the arrangements about so much they would have for their corn, their potatoes, and so forth.

And they would plow every day for so much a day, not by the hour. I don't think it was more than fifty cents a day at that time. And the old mules had to be taken care of. They'd have to get out the old mules every morning.

We had a farm bell, and they'd ring that bell every morning to get 'em [the workers] up, every morning about sunup. And they'd work all morning. Then they'd ring the bell about`11:30 for them to go home to dinner. And at 1:00 they'd have to come back and plow, no matter how long the days were. You know how long they are now. They'd plow all day long and never thought anything about it.

No, we didn't ring the bell at sundown. They knew to go home with the sun.

But they would come and they seemed to be so happy. They'd go across the field singing. I've missed that so much in later years. Just—they seemed so happy.

The cotton would be planted in long rows. They were really long. They would fix it all up in the spring and plant it about March. They had the planters. Mr. Litch made a cotton planter, you know. And so they used the Litch cotton planter; but, anyway, they'd fix it all, and it would be so pretty and so straight and so clean. Never a little bit of grass growing on the end like you see now.

When it began to come up, they'd watch it so careful, hoping that it would be a good stand. Then they'd cut it out with hoes, just go through it with the hoe and leave just a few stalks in a hill. But they don't do that anymore. They just let it go like it is.

And they'd plow it. Sometime in the summer they'd put a little bit of nitrate of soda to it, but never any more fertilizer. And it would grow so good.

And the same way with the corn. But they watched the cotton so carefully, you know, to see that no army worms or boll worms had got on it or anything.

It would begin opening about the last of August. I could remember because the household help always stopped at that time. Cooks and all went to picking cotton.

Everybody talked about how much this one was making and how much that—what the price was and all, till after Thanksgiving. If you were pretty smart, you had everything in by that time.

When you picked it, you had the bag to go over your shoulder. Tow sacks. They saved all the good tow sacks. And they'd have to be washed and put away. And they'd pick it into that. When you got one full, you put that one down and picked up another one. Then you'd carry them all to the end of the row and empty them on sheets.

And the man, the overseer or the man of the house, would take it and weigh it up.

And when they got it all on the big sheet, they'd bring the wagon in with the mules hitched to it. It was before the day of trucks. And those sheets would be tied up certain ways and certain loops. They had a loop over them to keep them from slipping. And they were loaded on the wagon and then taken to the gin. Early. Before day the next morning.

Well, the gin would knock the seeds out. The seeds would go in one place, cotton went in another. And then it would go on and get baled like it is now. They'd take it to a gin in town. There'd be gins dotted around all over the country.

They raised other things, too, but the cotton was so important at that time. Their main crop. It would mostly be in by around Thanksgiving, but there'd be a little scattering around after Christmas. But it would all be picked off. Wasn't none plowed under.

But the cotton crop was *the* crop. And I'll never forget, about in 1922 the boll weevil came. I'd never seen people so sick in my life. They were just ruined. Absolutely. Then later, they all got sprayers to spray for the boll weevil. And I remember my daddy saying—and he never did give up on anything—"Well, we're ruined now."

You see, the boll weevil would sting the boll; then it would rot. It wouldn't mature. It wouldn't open and mature. It was a little bug, about like a tiny cockroach.

MARY C. MC KINNON, 1886
Scotland County

Ginning Cotton by Water

My father had a cotton gin. And the way we first started ginning cotton was by water.

Well, the cotton, what we'd have to do in those days, we'd carry it to the gin. And they'd take it out in baskets and weigh it and you ginned the cotton for so much toll, like you would grind corn. So much per weight. Per hundred pounds. Then the cotton was put in what was known as a stall. And when the time come to gin it, they'd have to take it up again in baskets and carry it to the hopper of the gin. And it would be a very small gin in those days. You'd gin, probably, about four bales of cotton a day.

And you'd feed it into this gin. And you'd take your cotton, after it was ginned, you'd carry it to a press. That was a box. Drop your cotton in there. And they would pack it with their feet until it would get up to the top. They'd have two or three men in there packing. Just tramping on it with their feet, packing it down.

And after they would get the box full, they had levers that pulled down and pulled down. And they had what they called the dead man on top, and then they'd pull it down and press it into a bale. The dead man was what comes down on top of the box. No, it wasn't a man; it was like a top to the box, a press.

After it was pressed tight, they used cotton bands, metal bands that came around. And then when you fastened that thing, you released this rachet, and then you'd take this bale of cotton out. This band had a little buckle. You'd slip it in, and you'd press the end of the band in under next to the cotton and that would fasten it.

That's when we'd haul all the baled cotton to the wharf here and the boats would take it on down. That was after the railroad came. Before that it would go to Norfolk. Norfolk was the main port. You know, Norfolk was quite a port one time for cotton.

They had a belt to go from your water wheel and that would furnish you the power to turn your gin. The saws. The little saws go through ribs and pull the cotton. The seed won't go through, but the cotton will. You see, the cotton is a fiber, and that will string out and pull off the seed. Those little fingers were about an eighth inch apart. That was in the early days.

CHARLES L. REVELLE, SR., 1900
Hertford County

Growing Peanuts

I remember in those early days, before we had mechanical harvesting of peanuts, we had very limited acres planted in peanuts because we had no way of harvesting them. We had to plow those peanuts up with a mule and plow. And we'd go there and take those peanuts out of the ground and shake the dirt out of them, put them in little piles, and they would sun-dry for a day or two. Then we'd go back and pick those peanuts up and put them around a pole, and it was referred to as a "stack" of peanuts.

But in those days, after we'd put the peanuts around the stacks—we'd have small acreages—but the way we had to get the peanuts from the vine,

Osborne

we'd go to these stacks, or either pull these stacks up into a "hurdle," that is, several stacks together. And we'd have barrels. And we'd pick those peanuts from the vines by hand, or we'd have a barrel and we'd thrash them over the edge of the barrel and then we'd have to get the stems from them. And . . . in a day's time, you wouldn't get over a hundred or two pounds of peanuts. And, you know, if you had any acreage, it would take you quite a while in order to get a few hundred pounds of peanuts.

And a lot of people would get those peanuts off during and even at night; I've seen where they had lanterns they'd hang up and go out and pick those peanuts a lot of times in order to get them in before they damaged. The weather conditions would be so . . . you know, you couldn't let them stay there all the winter.

The way we cultivated was with a mule and plow, of course. And we planted, way back in the early days, by hand. That was before the planters came in. Then, in the early part of the century, they began to work on machinery, thrashing [threshing] machinery. The machine, actually the most successful machine, was invented by a man here in Murfreesboro.

We started that in the early teens. And those machines, to start with, what we had, were powered by using a horse. And they would go around with a long pole fastened to the machine, the horse would go around the machine, and that would turn the machine and would thrash the peanuts. And I remember very well, they'd have to have someone going along behind the horse to drive it, you know, to keep it going. Children sometimes did that. I've done it many a day.

After the machine came along, in the teens, we could plant more acres of peanuts. Prices were low. People lived at home in those days. We didn't know too much about going to a store to buy groceries or anything like that, except just the things we couldn't produce. Sugar, tea, salt, coffee. The other things we raised at home. And we lived at home.

We just had a minimum of clothes. Oh, I mean the clothes were all right, but they were work clothes, and we'd probably have a Sunday suit occasionally.

But we lived all right. It was a wonderful way of life. Of that time. We didn't expect a lot. And we enjoyed what we had. And we could have a good time with very little.

CHARLES L. REVELLE, SR., 1900
Hertford County

6   HAPPY TIMES   *Taking their enjoyment in simple pleasures, people around the turn of the century felt happiness to be mainly a state of mind. Fond memories center around childhood play. Families were large, and both games and playthings were usually homemade. Pleasant moments are recalled from evenings spent in lively talk around the stove in a country store. But the favorite form of social gathering seems to have been the "workings" when neighbors banded together in cooperative effort while fun and fellowship abounded.*

A Happier People

Oh,
I think
people were happier back then.

They didn't have
so much to worry over.

We had a big old dinner bell.
And everyday at dinnertime
they'd ring that bell
and
the horses would just whinker
out in the field.
Them horses knew they
were going to get their feed
when
we
did.

MAGGIE JEFFERS, 1894
ETHEL LUTZ, 1898
Cleveland County

Hiding in Cotton Baskets

One thing I want you to know: we had a big old basket 'bout like that [measures], made out of splits; and when it got cold, well, we never got no shoes till we picked the cotton and sold it.

And it'd be so cold I'd pick me a sack full and pour it in that basket and crawl down in it.

Every one of us had a basket and would crawl down in it.

Stayed there till Mother would ring the bell for us to come to dinner. Wouldn't have no cotton picked.

And back then we'd take sweet potatoes, and we'd pick so much and then get down in there and eat sweet potatoes and just have peelings all in the cotton.

Well, I'll tell you, there was seven of us girls and four boys and we really, especially the girls, really had a good time. Singing—go to the field a-singin' and come out a-singin'. Some of 'em sung alto and some tenor. You could hear us singin' out there before daylight.

MAGGIE JEFFERS, 1894
ETHEL LUTZ, 1898
Cleveland County

Parties of Young People

We didn't have cars like they do now. 'Course, there were some cars, but we young folks didn't have cars to just run up and down the road with. We walked. 'Course, I always seemed to have a way to go and a way to come back.

But we'd go stay all night. We'd just gang up from house to house, about six to eight of us, and go spend the night. We had the best times. There'd be a bunch of boys there and a bunch of girls. 'Course, the boys would go home before bedtime.

But there'd always be a certain number who were in love, would be courtin', and they'd just get them a spot over on the couch and sit real close together, you know. And they'd watch, but they didn't take no part in whatever was going on. And there was enough of us there who were just happy-go-lucky. That was . . . we'd keep everything going. Laughing, all kinds of old games, Spin-the-bottle and Post Office, which to us at that time was just the best time there ever was. 'Course, I guess these teenagers now would think we were crazy old coots, but we had a good time.

And we always loved to go over to Mr. Lester's. Mr. Lester couldn't hear good, you know. Papa would call "Bedtime," and Mr. Wall up here would call "Bedtime," but we could go over to Rosie Lester's, and we had the best time over there of anywhere. Her daddy couldn't hear good, so we could make all the racket we wanted to. And Mrs. Lester was the best cook of anybody in the group. She'd just get in that little old kitchen and cook and slave and fix the best food you ever eat in your life. And we'd eat just like we never had had nothing to eat before. Just like we were starving to death. Mr. Lester would just sit down in a chair and go to sleep or go to bed or something.

But I do remember one night about twelve or one o'clock we were down there, and Rosie kept saying, "Let's Charlie-Co!" Well, to me it wasn't a thing in the world except square dance. Charlie-Co . . . she said, "Let's Charlie-Co!" But, anyway, we got out on the floor, you know, everybody . . . and the old house was a-shaking. I guess maybe the sleepers or something were kindly loose; anyway, I know the floor was kindly shaking. We was just really living it up. We was just having the best time; you never heard such a noise in your life. 'Bout one o'clock Mr. Lester walked in. And Rosie just jumped back like she was scared to death. I guess it's the only time he ever come in to call us down.

He said, "You-all about finished?"

'Course, we all said, "Yes, sir."

And he said, "Well, I guess it's about time you stopped, then."

And Mrs. Lester said that was the only time anybody had ever offered to dance in her house. But it was her own daughter, Rosie, that wanted to do it.

'Most every night when we had a party, after the boys would go home, we'd go to bed. But when we went down to Mr. Lester's, we'd set up all night. I remember one night, there was eight of us. And it was one of the L-shaped houses with a hall in the middle, you know. Had the windows right over the front porch. And two of the girls took 'em a blanket and a pillow and went out that window, were going to sit out there on the housetop. And the rest of us was afraid to go to sleep, afraid they'd fall off, you know. And so we stayed up all night long.

And just before daylight—we had what we called a curling iron—and we'd hang 'em on the lamp chimney, or stick 'em down in the lamp chimney and let 'em get warm, and take 'em out and put 'em in our hair and roll it up. And that was the way we would curl it.

And so, along towards daylight awhile, we started curling hair. Them two still sitting out on the housetop. And we curled hair and we curled hair. Then about daylight it come a shower of rain and that dampness took every bit of the curl out.

But they came in when it rained. That brought 'em in.

And I remember one night in the winter-time, we spent the night down there. Woke up in the morning, and there was about a foot of snow on the ground. We didn't know how in the world we were going to get out from down in there. It was the end of the road. So we decided that whoever come first, we'd all come out with them, regardless.

It was way down, I guess a mile from anybody else, just way out down a steep little old hill to the house. But, when you got there, it was a real pretty place. It was so green-looking and cool down there, and just as clean. It was real pretty, but it was an out-of-the-way place to get to.

LUCY SPENCER, 1912
Stokes County

Pine Rosin Chewing Gum

Chewing gum
was something we discovered
after we were grown,
and . . . the earlier generations—
the first thing
we had to chew
was pine rosin.
Well, when the pine has been wounded,
the sap will come out of it.
And we used to take those little balls
and chew it.
That was the first chewing gum
I'm sure
many a soul here in eastern Carolina
ever had.
Had a pine taste.
Eventually
your teeth would become rather embroiled
in the whole thing.
And it got kind of sticky,
and you had to get rid of it
and find another wad.
But we loved to chew it,
and I'm sure we
were not the first generation
that did that.

LOUISE V. BOONE, 1922
Hertford County

Children's Games

Kids now don't, apparently, play like they used to. When I was a boy, we played Spin-the-bottle and ring games where we sang such songs as

"King David was King William's son;
Around the royal race he run . . . "

probably an old Scottish ring game, and

"Choose the one you love the best,"

and we'd select a young lady and—now, how did that go?

"And when you rise upon your feet,
Salute your bride and kiss her sweet."

That was the end of it, and that was really fine. And we played Hide-and-go-seek, and the boys played Roley Holey.

That was when you dug three little holes in the dirt in order, and then I believe there was another one off at an angle. And you shot marbles from hole to hole and tried to keep your opponent from getting ahead of you. You could shoot him and bounce his marble away off. And that, of course, caused him a lot of time and trouble and accuracy to get back in. I've forgotten exactly how it went, but we called it Roley Holey.

Now, there was, in Wilson County, out at Upper Town Creek, an old-fashioned marble court back in the old days where they used these big old alleys, a big old marble that was probably an inch to an inch and a half in diameter. And those were not shot; they were thrown. It was probably a variation of the English game of bowls or something like that where they used those great big balls five or six inches in diameter.

Now, in this game, you would throw your marbles at certain marbles that were placed in a ring or some position in the court. There was a background, sort of a board background, so that you couldn't throw out of bounds, reasonably.

And they were playing marbles out there that old-fashioned way until around thirty years ago. But I think that died out when the older ones who enjoyed it died out or got too old.

HUGH B. JOHNSTON, JR., 1913
Wilson County

Town Ball and Peg

We used to play Town Ball, and for a bat we used a paddle to hit our ball with, made like an oar out of white oak. It was very heavy.

And we played Peg. We had a peg about that long, and put about that much up on this fulcrum, see? And hit it with a stick and made it fly up here and then hit it with a stick again and counted the distance we knocked it.

And it was a pretty good game. We got a lot of exercise out of it.

LEE EDWIN KISER, D.C., 1898
Iredell County

Yes, the one that hit it would say, "I'll give you twenty-five jumps," or ten or whatever. Then the other boys would try to jump to it in that number of jumps. If one of them did it, he got the points. Otherwise, the batter collected the points, and the first one to a hundred won.

WORFORD R. SPENCER, 1905
Stokes County

Foot Races

Back in those days,
there were
big families of children—
ten, twelve, or more.
But there were just five
in our family.

All the children in the neighborhood
would get together
over at the "Race Track."

That's what we called the old playground
that was near
where the old slave cabins
used to be.

So,
we'd all meet up there
and have foot races
and
all other different kinds
of races and games.

WORFORD R. SPENCER, 1905
Stokes County

Sledding

And then
we had boards over there,
to the north of Creason.

We'd get on a plank,
and we weren't afraid of those trees . . .
we were goin' to go through
down at the bottom of the hill.

We knew we weren't going to hit 'em.

We'd be just a-flying.

Just riding a plank
like a sled,
a bobsled.

Oh, yeah,
it was frozen.

LEE EDWIN KISER, D.C., 1898
Iredell County

Corncob Battles

Then,
we'd have corncob battles
up at my dad's,
you see.

Those of us in the loft
didn't have to have as big a force
as those on the bottom
because we had a little advantage.

It was all right
as long
as nobody soaked their corncobs.

Once you got it wet,
why,
you could do a little damage with it.

I remember
Henry got hit one time,
hurt pretty bad,
and he started home,

but
we persuaded him not to go.

He got hit with a wet corncob.

LEE EDWIN KISER, D.C., 1898
Iredell County

Tom Walkers

Another thing
we did
was
walk
on tom walkers.

but
mostly
up the creek.

We went
everywhere
on
them,

They
were
like stilts.

WORFORD R. SPENCER, 1905
Stokes County

Going to the Store

When I think back,
it seems like a long, long time ago.

I remember we used to go
down to the store
every night.

That was a regular hangout
for everybody in this neighborhood.

Didn't matter how dark,
how cold the weather was,
we'd all try to get down there.

Just an old country store.

Sold everything from pickles to shoes.
Pretty good line of shoes, too.

'Course, we didn't go to buy
anything, 'specially.

We just went.

LUCY SPENCER, 1912
Stokes County

Corn Shuckings

Well, now, I was just a young girl, but I enjoyed it just as much as the women did. Evidently they just invited all the neighbors. They had sort of a group that always worked together. When Papa had a corn shucking, every man for miles around came. And about four or five women would come and help cook.

And, oh boy, those big old pots of chicken and dumplings! Great big old three-, four-gallon potfuls, you know. And they cooked a big old pot of beans. Everything that was cooked—see, this was all on a wood stove—everything was in great big pots, and it was so good! I could just eat and eat and eat.

And, of course, those men would try to outeat each other. It would take the awfulest potfuls to feed them. Usually they'd just eat dinner and go home before night. But I have known them to stay on and eat supper, too.

Oh, yes, they'd start in the morning. And it'd be in the wintertime when the days weren't so long. Just as soon as the sun got up a little bit, they'd get out there and start shucking. And they'd just shuck all day long.

But it was fun. They had a good time. You know, Papa had just hauled the corn up and piled it off in a big pile. He'd just bring it up on the wagon and rake it off there. Well, there was just a semicircle all the way 'round, you know. And I guess they sat on the ground, or boxes, or buckets, or whatever—maybe some of them brought their chair with them. But it would just be that big circle of men around that big old pile of corn, you know—and they could shuck corn!

They usually had it right in front of the crib, and everybody just threw his ear of corn at the crib, trying to hit the door. Part of it hit the door and part of it didn't.

And, when they got through—if they got through before night, and if they didn't, the family had it to do the next morning—they had what they called a shuck pen, and everybody had to go get up the shucks, just get these great big armfuls and dump 'em in. The shuck pen was made out of split rails, a big round pen, and that's what they put the shucks in.

I guess all those old split rails just finally rotted away. The shucks they fed to the cows.

LUCY SPENCER, 1912
Stokes County

Quiltings

We used to have them at home. Out in the back house here, I still have the clamps and the rails that they sewed them onto. But these ladies would get together in the springtime when the days were getting longer.

"Well, there's going to be a quilting over at the McKinnons." And the neighborhood would be invited. Well, if it was to be at my mother's house, she'd start immediately making pies and cakes and fixing up, boil a ham . . . food was plentiful. So then they'd come and they'd have their thimbles and a certain kind of needle, if they wanted it. The thread would be furnished, and the quilt would be in the frame.

They had chairs that they used in the quilting. Some of our chairs are out here on the front porch now. They're homemade. And they were all of the same size and they would not slide around. They're flat. So they had those and put one in each corner, the size of the quilt. And they'd put those frames up and stretch them as far as they could. Then they would clamp that down with an iron clamp. The two sides would be sewn in. The two sides would be fixed, but the ends were not. But then they would have everything

laid in there, but that would be before the folks would get there, however. And they would put in the batting. They had carded the batting by hand. They would pick the finest kind of cotton and pick it over and card it.

And when they got the cotton laid in, they'd pull over the top—stretch it as far as they could and tack it down. And then they were ready to quilt.

My mother just had certain people that she wanted to quilt with. The average one makes too long a stitches. Or maybe they didn't go all the way through, sometimes. You know, you've got to go all the way through.

And they had certain designs to use in the quilting, in the sewing. They had a shell design; and then they sometimes did it by the piece. If they were small, you know, they'd go around each piece. But if it was a comfort or anything, they usually made shells, or even kind of go across them and make a log cabin.

Now, the tops had designs, too. They had the patchwork, and then they had the piece quilts. One real pretty one that my mother had was the "Cactus." It was the most beautiful work. Sister had a "Save All" quilt. It was cut out, one color, and then that would leave the space, and you could fit in every bit of it. That was the name of the pattern. "Save All." There wasn't any waste about it. It made kind of a chain, like. But there were so many, many patterns.

Sometimes they had as many as three or four quilts. And they would sit down and chat. That was the way they spent their time, you know. Gossiping. Talked about everything. And when noontime came, they would all be called out for lunch.

And, oh, all the good food people did have. Just everything you could think of. After dinner they'd come back and quilt. And most of the time they got the quilt out.

But there was one lady who lived over here . . . well, when they finished quilting, she got out the shirts for them to mend. She was that thrifty. And that was . . . interesting . . . to the ones who went. They didn't get to relax at all, because she got the shirts out.

MARY C. MC KINNON, 1886
Scotland County

Wood Choppings

And they had the wood choppings in the spring. All the men came and brought their axes. Some of them might have brought a crosscut saw.

At that time, they didn't know what a chain saw was. And, of course, the women did the cooking just like they did for the corn shucking. But the men would get out there and cut enough wood to last all year curing tobacco and fireplace wood and stovewood.

But we had good times. And each woman knew what she could cook best. Miss Ollie would cook a rice pudding, and I declare she could make the best 'uns I ever ate. She was real good on rice puddings. And, maybe, one could bake better bread, and somebody else could make better pies, something like apple pies, or those old big pan pies, you know. Fruit pies. Law! That was good eating!

But that chicken and dumplings and those pinto beans were my favorite! 'Course, they had mashed potatoes. Everything that grew on the farm.

You could just put that big old hunk of meat in those pinto beans and set them back on the stove and let 'em cook a long time. Ellis and Clyde would sit over here on the bench behind this table and eat pinto beans and laugh.

I'll never forget it. Clyde always loved the big old hunk of meat that was boiled in the pintos, you know. And I remember one day he said he had eat more pinto beans than he wanted a many a time just to get that fat meat they were cooked with. But he said he hated to just reach back and get more meat when he didn't get more beans. Sometimes it would be meat on the bone, and sometimes it would be just regular old middlin' meat—pork. A ham bone gave it better flavor.

LUCY SPENCER, 1912
Stokes County

Peanut Poppings

And then we had what we called peanut poppings, to shell the peanuts for planting purposes. We always had to shell the seed for planting. And then they would gather at this house, maybe tonight. And there would be fifteen or twenty people there. And they'd go and pop peanuts for that person. And maybe a few nights later they'd have it at another person's.

And they would have a sugar pull. Get two people to pull and stretch it. And you had that at the same time as the peanut popping. That was part of the fun that went along with it. It was the kind of stuff that made this hard work—well, it added a little fun to it.

Practically every week there was something like this going on. It didn't become boring at all. You were busy; you worked hard. Then you played. You didn't have the entertainment; you made your own entertainment. That was all. You enjoyed each other. Visited with each other.

Their neighbors were all they knew. They didn't know anybody else other than somebody around, maybe, in a radius of five or ten miles. They had no way to travel other than by horse and buggy. Or horse and cart. That's the only way we traveled.

CHARLES L. REVELLE, SR., 1900
Hertford County

Cotton Pickings

In the fall it's nice. But when it gets cold, it gets harder to pick. And your fingers get cold picking, too. You'd start in September, but I'd say the middle of October or the middle of November was the main months. 'Course, we have picked all winter on days when it was warm enough, if you didn't get done. It'd get so cold you couldn't pick cotton. Fingers would get cold and your feet. You wasn't moving enough to keep your body warm.

If it rained and the cotton got wet, then you had to wait till it got dry.

Lot of people, when it would get cold, would pull the whole boll off and bring it in the house to the fire and have a cotton picking. The neighbors would come in and help you, and, of course, the young people got in one room and the older folks in another.

Chicken pie! Everything you could think of. Big dinners. You threw the burrs in the fire to make light. 'Course, you didn't care whether there was too much light or not.

Now, about all those big dinners. They'd cook big chicken pot pies in a great big aluminum dish pan. Great big. Fill up the oven full. Cooked everything you could think of. And everyone was hungry. They'd just eat like they were starved. Just like a workin'.

CARME ELAM, 1896
CLEO ELAM, 1902
Cleveland County

7 HARD TIMES

In all aspects of life, people cared for themselves and for one another, from birth to death. Relying solely on their own ingenuity, they met life's great moments with fortitude, knowing that when the time comes, one simply does what has to be done.

Birth

Well,   would
we seemed   get there,
to get along
pretty well.   and
                            sometimes
Sometimes   he
the doctor   wouldn't.

MINNIE LEE SPENCER, 1879
Stokes County

Assisting at Childbirth

But I never lost a baby. I would go and help them through every minute of it. Usually me and the doctor, if he made it. Sometimes, just me and another woman. We'd take care of the baby and the mother, too. We'd just fix them all up. Sometimes we'd have them all fixed when the doctor got there. If I was by myself, and the baby got there, I'd wrap it all up snug, but I wouldn't cut the cord. I'd wait till the doctor got there and let him do that. I never would do that.

Why, I've seen those little old bright eyes just looking up at me, just as bright as you've ever seen. I'd just wrap them up in a cloth and wait till he got there. I've been with women that sure did suffer, too. Sometimes we'd use chloroform—hold it to their nose sometimes. I was the one who had to hold it, and it got me. But it always seemed to come along all right.

Now, I had one doctor to use forceps. I didn't like that, not at all. But she was a young woman, and that was her first one and the doctor said that would hasten up the time. I told him I didn't like that, that I'd never used anything like that. She got along all right, and they were both still living the last I knowed of them.

And I went out at night a lot of times. Well, you see, a heap of times they'd ask me before-hand. And it'd just be a-snowing or a-raining, but I'd lay a dress out, because I'd know I might have to get up. And sometimes it'd be thataway; I'd just have to go through the rain or the snow. They usually didn't wait for me; they'd just let me know. Well, if it was some of our own folks around here, I'd go back with them. But usually Bud would get up and go with me, and then he'd come back home.

A good part of the time—well, Forest had got him one of these little old runabout cars, you know—and they'd come for Forest to go after the doctor and me to come for them. And we done that, I don't know how long.

Oh, they'd offer to pay me, but I never took a cent. Never one time in my life. I wouldn't charge them anything.

Sometimes they'd come after me in a two-horse wagon. Then, later on, they'd come in a car. But I didn't charge them a cent and never would have a cent.

One time when one of my children was born, Bud went after the doctor and he couldn't come. He was sick. And Bud come back home. He had to go on horses then. Come back home and told me, "He said he can't come. What must I do? He said if you didn't get along all right, he'd come by six o'clock in the morning."

"Well," I said, "You'd better stay here." I knowed there wasn't another doctor any closer than Danbury then. "You'd better be here, 'cause I might need you." And that was when Forest was born. Sure enough, the child was born, and there wasn't a soul here except me and him and Ellie. Ellen Rhodes up here. She's awful good. She'd take children and fix them same as the doctor would. But she said if that had been her and her husband had come in and told her anything like Bud told me, it would have scared her to death.

Well, there wasn't too much to do. When I went out, I always took me a band and a scorched cloth, and I'd put that scorched cloth right on that part of the cord that was left, and then fastened that band all around it right good and tight. The doctor had told me to pin it just as tight as I could, except I would keep two fingers under it. And then I'd wash and fix the child and dress him. And then fix up the mamma. Then clean up everything.

Why, yes, we got along all right without a doctor, but we always liked to have one, anyway. He didn't have much to do sometimes. But other times, he'd have a right smart job. And that doctor didn't charge but two or three dollars. Our doctor was Dr. Ellington, the one who came to me with every child I ever had, except that one. He never did charge us over three dollars, as I remember.

And then, after these children were born, I always went around to see them, to see if they were getting along all right. If something was a little wrong, they'd send for me, just the same as they did for the doctor. And I'd go to them and do everything I could.

Now when one little boy out here was born, we had a young doctor from Walnut Cove. I don't know what his name was, but he just took a piece of webbing and wound right around that child's waist and right around his navel and didn't put nothing else on him, just wound that thing all around him. And, I guess it was a day or so later, they sent for me, said the child was crying and they didn't know what to do. They wanted me to come out there and see what to do for him. So I went out and I took the scissors and cut that thing off and put my band back on it like always, and he got along all right. Hushed his crying. But as a common thing, we just put that scorched cloth and band on one, after we greased it a little bit to keep it from sticking. We greased it with a little salve.

We got cloths and made diapers and pinned them on and put a little shirt on them and a flannel slip. I put flannel slips on every child of mine. And another one over that, then its dress. And its dress went down yonder about a yard long. Boys and girls. They all wore dresses. I kept them things on my babies about three months, then I put on a short dress down around their feet.

And when the little boys were about a year old, we put little pants on them. Or sometimes they wore little aprons or dresses. One of mine wore his red flannel all the summer.

MINNIE LEE SPENCER, 1879
Stokes County

Twelve Children and No Doctor

My mother had twelve children and never had a doctor. Sufferin', said hadn't nobody suffered like she did. When she was going to have a baby, she'd send every one of us off. Wouldn't tell us one thing in the world. She'd hide the clothes that she was makin' for the baby. She'd always send us over to our aunt's, and she'd tell us that they got the baby out of the closet.

And she'd have the baby one white—oh, it was beautiful, white flannel and two red ones. Long, 'bout that long. And she had a little trunk and kept it locked. Kept 'em in that trunk. Two little red ones for everyday, and the white one was for Sunday. And I always thought they was just the prettiest—that was the prettiest flannel I thought I'd ever seen.

They couldn't keep 'em dry. My mother would tear up old shirts and shirt tails and make diapers out of 'em. You just didn't have the money. All the diapers you bought, you just bought the cotton flannel and hemmed 'em all around and they was for Sunday.

When I was a child, I'd go with my mother places and see mothers sit up to the fireplaces, if it was in the wintertime, and have their babies on their laps with that long dress to the fire to dry. Just had 'em up to the fire.

MAGGIE JEFFERS, 1894
ETHEL LUTZ, 1898
Cleveland County

No Undertaker

Well,
when anybody died,
we went to 'em,

and we made the shrouds
and fixed 'em

and dressed 'em
and put 'em in their coffin
and buried 'em.

There was no undertaker about it.

MINNIE LEE SPENCER, 1879
Stokes County

Preparations for Burial

Well, we just bought a coffin, you know. And there wasn't a thing in the world in that coffin only a little piece like hamburg tacked around here for to swing down on the inside. The bottom was naked. Just plain naked.

When Bud's mammy died, Jennie says to

me, she says, "I don't want her put in that old hard box with nothing under her. Will you make a bed and put in there for us to put her on?"

I told her, "Yes." She said she had cotton all ready. Well, she went and got some cotton and some bleachin' [white domestic cloth], and I made her a bed and put in that coffin and we laid her on it. Fixed a pillow under her head and put her on that bed.

Everybody else had the idea to just put 'em right in that hard box. Never put nothing else in it.

Well, when anybody died, we went to 'em, and we made the shrouds and we fixed 'em, and dressed 'em and put 'em in their coffin and buried 'em. There was no undertaker about it.

No money about it. We didn't charge anybody a cent for what we done. We done everything free.

Over their face, we'd take a piece of cloth, maybe that big square [measures with hands] and the way I notched it around the edge, they called it dovetailed. I made a many a one. That was always spread over their face. Didn't put nothing else over them. Only their clothes. Just washed them and put clean clothes on them. We always washed the one that died, just washed 'em good. There wasn't anything we could do to 'em to make 'em look no better. Just had to bury 'em like they looked.

Who made the coffins? They made 'em down here at Jim Shelton's. Made 'em around different places. But down here at Sandy Ridge, Jim Shelton had a place, you know, where he made furniture. And he made them coffins a long time there. Just good strong oak wood, walnut, whatever you wanted thataway.

How much did they cost? Oh, about ten or fifteen dollars. Something like that. They finally went up a little bit higher, but ten dollars would get a nice one. They painted 'em, made 'em nice. Dressed 'em good on the outside. Painted 'em real dark mahogany, brown, something like that. I never saw no other colors.

Babies? They made 'em just the same way. Made 'em a little coffin, just the size you want. You just say the length and the width, however you wanted, a little person or a big person, just big enough for to put 'em in good. They made it. You had to let 'em know. They kept some. You could go in and see if they had one like you wanted. But, if not, it didn't take long to make 'em.

We'd keep 'em up about three days. Three days just like they do now. But if something happened so they couldn't get 'em to the place to bury 'em on time, they'd sometimes wait longer, but three days, as a regular thing. Now, Christ, you know, was in his grave three days. I guess that's where it come from.

But now, my mammy said her mammy, they had to keep her up a week on account of the river being up. They had to go across the river to get to the graveyard where they were going to bury her.

We used to have to cross the river *in it*; there wasn't no bridges, you know, much. That was in Rockingham. Had to ford it. But they finally got across.

Now, my great-grandpa Drewry drowned down here in the river. Someone on the other side saw him when he was trying to get across and drowned. And they got him out, but he was already drowned.

And his horse would go back and forth across the river. You know, it washed him off'n his horse. His horse would go back and forth and nicker after he was washed off it. It was his riding horse, the one he was always used to.

Law, people had bad times getting across rivers then.

We just kept 'em at home and set up with 'em when they died, until they were buried.

People just came in and set up with us. Why, we didn't have no funeral home till here of late.

Now, my mammy and pappy both joined the funeral home right after they started it up, and it wasn't long till they died. You know, you could join up with it, and they'd give you a hundred dollars off the cost when you died.

Martin Hawley down here, his wife belonged to it when she died, and he said it didn't cost him but ten cents to bury her. Ten cents. That's all it cost him. But now look what it costs.

When my uncle's little child died, I guess it was maybe eight or nine months old, they come to me. I was still a young girl at my daddy's, before I was married. They come to me and wanted me to make that child a shroud.

Well, I didn't know a thing in the world about what size, or how to cut a pattern or nothing about it. But I cut that dress and made it and fixed it and put it on that child. He was as pretty a little child as I ever seen.

It was a white dress, white lace and baby blue ribbon. And I made it and gathered the little sleeves, you know, put lace on the sleeves, gathered the band and put ribbon, made a bow on each sleeve and fixed the neck with the lace and ribbon. I can't remember exactly just how I put the trimming on the neck now. But I trimmed it.

Why, it fitted just as good as if I'd had all kinds of patterns.

MINNIE LEE SPENCER, 1879
Stokes County

Training in Burial Customs

"Lelia, did people have preservatives to use on the body when a person died?"

"No, I don't know as they did. Turpentine or camphor cloth on their face. That would keep them from changing. But they'd bathe them off good first, then they'd straighten them out as straight as they could and close their eyes and put money on them to hold them together, you know. And after they got them dressed and their hair combed, they fixed them up with this weight stuff, money mostly. Just a quarter or a fifty cents on the eyes; then they would wet a cloth in turpentine or camphor to keep 'em from changing."

"What do you mean, changing?"

"Well, they would turn dark and look terrible bad, but this . . . it was all the embalming fluid they had then, was camphor, and that was made out of gum camphor and liquor. Pure liquor. And you shaved that up and put it in the bottle. Have you ever seen camphor? People made their own, way back yonder."

"And how did they make it?"

"Well, they'd take camphor gum; you buy it and it looks like paraffin. But it's got the camphor smell, and they'd shave that up and put it in a bottle. My mama's—I'd give anything for the camphor bottle that my mama had. It was a hair-tonic bottle, I reckon. It was blue. It was the prettiest-shaped thing and had a neck on it and a glass stopper in the top, you know; and it always set on the mantel. That's about the only medicine you had back then. I've seen her rub her temples and forehead and put it across her nose whenever she had the headache. It'll stop the headache, you know.

"And so they'd take a white cloth and wet it with camphor. And every once in a while, they'd take and wet it again and lay it over the face of the dead until they carried them to the church. But a lot of folks had the cemeteries right at home. They'd have the funerals right at home, then carry them out to the cemetery and bury them.

"My older brother said no wonder it was so horrible then. Now and they fix 'em til they don't look like they're dead. It's a whole lot easier on them now. You know, they used to have their mouths open and their eyes—sometimes you couldn't get 'em to close atall. Just looked horrible and just hurt you worse'n . . . Now'n they just look like they're asleep.

"But then, too, there was the cooling board. That's what they used . . . it was a wide plank, you know, and they laid 'em on that after they got 'em dressed, before they put 'em in the coffin. And that's when they'd get stiff. Well, they tried to get 'em washed and dressed before they got stiff, if they could. See, you could get their arms around better. After they got stiff you couldn't do much with 'em. You couldn't move 'em around. Yeah, they'll begin getting stiff in two or three hours. So you really have to work pretty fast. And when they got 'em fixed, they'd lay 'em on the cooling board. Maybe they didn't get the casket until the next day, or they didn't get it made, you see. And then they'd cover 'em up with a sheet."

"Now, what about the caskets? Did they make them at home?"

"Oh, yes, they'd make 'em. I don't remember hearing 'em make one, but I've known of makin' 'em. My daddy helped make a many a one because he run the roller mill. And they always used to have wide planks. Had big timber. Trees

were bigger. They're all cut down now, you know. And then they was big enough. Had one deep plank for the side and one for the bottom. Yes, sir. Wide enough. They would cut 'em off square and then they'd, where the shoulders was, they'd be a little bit wider. They'd cut the bottom, and then they'd cut that other plank to fit. They came out like that, and then they went down, tapered, for the feet. Just like an old casket. Coffin. That's what they were—coffins."

"And did they put that inside another one?"

"Well, maybe they did. Maybe then they just had a straight one. But I imagine they just put it right in the ground, like it was."

"And did they line the coffin?"

"Well, they had quilts or blankets or something like that to lay them on. They usually tried to put a pillow in under the head."

"Must have been a sad business."

"Yes sir! Well, I've helped lay out two or three dead people myself. Miss Maude Clayton, I helped bathe her and dress her. And William Manning, too.

"But anyway, Mable's baby died when they lived down there below us, and so they wanted me to come and fix it, or help to; and Frank went to King and got the casket. It was just an infant, wasn't very old. And so I fixed it and laid it in there, and we went on with them to the funeral down at Peter's Springs. And I went up and took the top off and they all come around and looked at it. Now, they just kept the outside of the coffin natural. They generally kept some pretty white forest pine to make 'em out of. No they didn't have time to paint them.

"We've come a long ways, and yet we're right back where we started, in a way.

"It was hard; but always people would turn loose and go then, you know. And when anybody got sick, they didn't have a hospital to carry them to, so people would just go and sit up at night. And when anybody died, they'd sit up all night, too. Somebody stayed in the room with the body all the time.

"You know, I think of these families who used to live so far off from their nearest neighbor, and they couldn't get the word out, so they just had to do it all themselves.

"But, you see, they were taught then. They had come from England and Scotland and all over in there over here, and they had learned it over there. It just kindly goes in families to do one thing and some do another.

"I'll tell you, our forefathers had it pretty rough, trying to fix a way for us, didn't they?"

LELIA F. BAKER, 1903
visiting with Patsy M. Ginns, Stokes County

Criminal Flees

Usually,
when
a man committed
a crime,
such as killing someone,
he would leave.
He'd just go off
and stay
years and years

and then
maybe
sometimes
he'd come back home

when
he was
real old.

LUCY SPENCER, 1912
Stokes County

Hiding Out

That's the way they used to do. We knew of this family who lived alone, just the mammy and a big crowd of children. Their daddy had killed a man, but, instead of leaving, he was hiding out.

The house had a plank walk out in front, just loose boards laid side by side, leading up to the door; and you could hear somebody coming on the planks because they'd make a noise when you'd step on them.

The wife would lie awake at night and listen for her husband's footsteps on the planks. He had the reputation of being a violent, mean man, and the children were deathly afraid of him. The wife may have been, too, but she couldn't help herself.

Although he was hiding out, he'd come in at night sometimes to get food and fresh clothes. The family would go to bed and listen for the planks to rattle.

LUCY SPENCER, 1912
Stokes County

Family Tragedy

There were two brothers, and one of the brothers had lost his wife. And one of his two little sons died, and that just left him with one surviving son. He hired a housekeeper, and, apparently, the housekeeper was a young woman of rather loose reputation.

In the family I think they had a pretty good idea that Uncle Ed was sort of carrying on with the housekeeper, really, in sort of an unsanctified relationship.

And Uncle John, who had fought in the Civil War . . . was one of the family who had some words with him about the situation. The Farmer family were considerable land owners in the area, and they were a very highly thought of, highly respected family.

The two brothers, apparently, both had something of a taste for alcohol, and they were over at a political rally, and it was in 1880, about October. They had both been drinking and had some words. Friends had gotten them separated and gotten one of them off in one direction and the other off in another.

But Uncle John went to his mother's home. The old house is still standing, but it's deserted now, built in 1860. He went to his mother's home, and it was cool so they were all in by the fire. But Uncle John went out to the well when Uncle Ed came up, apparently with a musket. It was supposed to have been the same musket that Uncle John had brought back from the Civil War. But, at any rate, they had words out there by the well, and the rest inside could hear some of the higher tones. And then there was a shot. But nobody went out.

And in a few minutes, a neighbor came over and found Uncle John lying by the well dead as a hammer. He had been shot at close range because the shot and wadding were all lodged under his heart.

Well, they sent word into town immediately for the sheriff and the coroner, and they said they would be out the next morning. Well, Uncle John lay there by the well all night under a sheet or blanket or something until the coroner came. There was no question about what had happened. Uncle Ed had shot his brother to death. And the tracks led out across the field to the branch and the woods, so there was no question about which direction he had gone.

Well, for two or three days the sheriff's department tried to find Edwin Barnes Farmer, but a friend had carried blankets to him, and food, and was helping him get ready to leave. Keep out of sight.

And so, after a few days, he put a little trunk on the back of a horse, and he departed by night. And from that day to this, the family has never heard one word about what became of him. Of course, he's long since dead. But that was the end of him.

Well, you can imagine the sensation it was in the Toisnot Township area and what a terrible tragedy it was in the family.

Now, John Farmer, who was killed, left five or six small children; and Uncle Ed, of course, left only one.

Now, this happened in 1880, and it's no reflection against me or anybody else. It's just one of those things similar to what happened in a great many families. Things like this were not peculiar to any particular social group. It happened to some of the most solid people in the community as well as some of the most disreputable.

HUGH B. JOHNSTON, JR., 1913
Wilson County

Hanging

They hung two of the robbers and invited the public. It was out in front of the courthouse. And they always built the scaffold. 'Course, they didn't have a parking lot there then.

Anyway, our oldest brother went. Papa took him. And I know Mother said, well, she kinda shook her head, but they let him go to see a hanging. But he didn't say much about it. It kinda made him sick.

I was about ten years old. And I was born in 1890 so it was about 1900. That was all we heard for months.

They hung two of 'em. One's name was Jessup and the other was Gunther. And then there was two others, and I can't think of their names, but they gave them life. But four of them, now, going there to rob that tiny little post office. That's where we got our mail.

FRANCES C. COLE, 1890
Buncombe County

A Sad Time

I've always thought
it was the nearest thing to death
that I've ever seen,
to see a house burn down.

I've always thought
that anybody who sees a house burn,
it does something to them.

It's the saddest time.

I guess it's just seeing
everything you've got,
everything you've worked for,
and the things you treasure . . .
the things that could never be replaced

just burned up.

LUCY SPENCER, 1912
Stokes County

A Home Burns

That chair over there is homemade. It's my grandmother's chair. It's been sawed off. Practically every grandchild that comes here wants that chair. They all want it. It's the only homemade one I've got. But I say, "Well, I'll let it set here. You all can bid on it the day of the sale."

Now, Gabe and his daddy both used to make stools. But all the old things burnt up when the house burned. 1933. Wasn't nobody there except me and my two boys. Gabe had gone to Wes Moorefield's over yonder next to North View. Everything burned up.

We'd washed and ironed and cleaned up for Christmas, me and Lelia had. And had our clothes, just got through ironing that day, had them all packed up clean.

Lamp full of oil caught afire in Lelia's room. The back room was just burnt through the top when I found it. Lelia went home with Cora, and I was a-making me an apron. Well, the lamp went out in my room, and I kept a-hearing something knocking, and I reckon I always was one to be afraid, and I just thought that it was somebody a-fooling with me. Well, I got up and went into the kitchen and didn't see no light or nothing in there, and I went back in the house and the light went out in the fireplace. Well, I says, there's somebody around here somewhere's. So I went back out in the lower porch and I seen the blaze going out the top of the house.

Colin was eleven years old, and Leland was nine. Both of 'em was in the bed asleep, and I had to get 'em out. I called Colin. Waked him up. I says, "Get up. The house is afire; we got to get out." And I says, "Get up, Leland!" I knowed he was hard to wake up.

I picked him up and set him out in the floor, and he jerked aloose from me and said, "Ma, I'm sleepy!" and jumped back in the bed.

I said, "Leland, the house is a-burning up, son! You'll burn up. We've got to get out!"

He jumped back out on that floor and said, "How? Where is it a-burning at?"

And I says, "Back there in the back room." He got up when he waked.

Well, I took them down there and set them under a apple tree, and I told them not to come back to the house. Then I went back and started toting out things until the joists began to fall in. I was there by myself. And I hollered. And I rung the bell. I reckon I was scared, 'cause I jerked it too hard and it hung. And I hollered three times just as loud as I could holler.

Walter and Rachel come. I reckon they seen the fire.

I got out the sewing machine and two or three chairs, and what clothes was on the bed downstairs. And I picked—you know, I was scared—I picked the bed up and started out the door with it, and it hit the door frame. It was a iron bedstead. I picked the whole thing up there and started out the door with it. I had picked the sewing machine up and toted it out in the yard. And I'd been walking with a cane that day. I'd been so weak I couldn't hardly walk. I got some things.

I got the children's clothes. Gabe had got them a pair of high-topped shoes that day—everyday shoes. And they thought so much of 'em. And they wanted them. They come back to the house and got them. That's the only time they came back.

And Lelia, she come when she heard me holler. She was just down . . . and she was going upstairs. And they had to hold her. She said all of her clothes was upstairs. I says, "Lelia, they're burning up." I says, "Just be thankful, Lelia, they ain't no flesh a-burning." I says, "Maybe we can work someway to get some more clothes."

It just liked to have killed her. She said we just couldn't live. But I says, "Why, Lelia, we'll get something."

It was a house of two rooms and a pantry. They called it a pantry where they kept the flour and meal and stuff in between the house, and two porches. And the kitchen. Two rooms upstairs.

I sat out there on the bench and watched the sweet 'taters drop down the steps; here went the preserves. They all dropped down the steps. Gabe's gun fired one barrel at the time, just like somebody was shooting it.

OLLIE HALL, 1896
Stokes County

Ice for Typhoid Victims

When I was a boy, we had an ice pond. We had a icehouse. There was quite a bit of typhoid fever at that time, and they needed ice. They packed 'em in ice. We furnished the ice free.

They used it to cool 'em off, in sacks. Crush it and put it in sacks to cool the fever, see? Pretty large percentage of 'em died. My grandmother and my mother's oldest sister died of typhoid fever. My aunt died, and then the next day, or the second day, my grandfather died.

And we put ice out there in the icehouse. And it'd be four to six inches thick, and we'd saw it out about four feet long. They'd pile it on up in there, 17½ feet deep, it was. And then, on up above the ground, they used sawdust for insulation.

And you'd walk up in there on the ice, and of course, when you put hot crocks of milk in there, why, they'd make an indentation in the ice, and it'd never turn over. You'd go put it back in the same place.

We had cold watermelons in there, and mushmelons. At that time we didn't know anything about cantaloupes.

Years later, the only ice we could get would be shipped up there in sacks with sawdust in between the sacks, come by train to King. Our winters got to where we didn't have four-inch ice.

We did have cold weather back there before then, though. I've heard people tell of driving teams across Catawba River on ice.

LEE EDWIN KISER, D.C., 1898
Iredell County

Typhoid Epidemic

I was six years old when my mammy died. Me and my brother was taken with typhoid fever. I can recollect how, when Mama was taken sick, how I always went with her to milk and toted the bucket. And I got up nearly to milk and she called me and told me she couldn't come, for me to come back.

That was about 1902. Yes, it was 1902, because my little sister was six weeks old when Mama died, and she was born in 1902. My sister Cora stayed with my aunt till we got up from the fever. I had it, too. I don't know how long it lasted, but it was a right smart while. Uncle Henry was down with it, and Hal and me. All three of us. Uncle Henry took a backset, and he was bad off for a long time.

The doctor come every day. I'll never forget that. I was just six years old, but I remember that. Typhoid fever was what Dr. Ellington called it.

Now, how come our grandmother to get it, Harold Dean married my mother's sister, and he lived at Mayodan. And Aunt Sally took it and died. And he had three boys and wanted to come back to Grandma Shelton's. And they took him back, then they took the fever. My grandmother took it, and our mother went and waited on her, then Mama took it, and she died, too.

And my Grandmother Shelton got better, so when we all got up from the fever, we went and stayed with her. While we had the fever, we stayed at Grandpa Hawkin's, Pa's daddy.

And it was a year. We wasn't down that long, but Law! we was so weak. You were so weak that—why, they wouldn't let you eat nothing! I don't know why. The doctor wouldn't let us have nothing. I got up so I could walk, and you nearly perished to death.

Well, they would let us have some soup, a little bit of soup. Wasn't nary bit of grease about it, though. And Uncle Henry wanted something to eat. He couldn't set up. And he told me to go to the—they had a cupboard in his room, one of these old-timey cupboards, and they had the light bread in there they give 'em, homemade light bread in the cupboard—and he told me to go and get him that plate of light bread and hand it to him. I went and got it and give it to him. And he eat all he wanted.

He said, "Now, Ollie, you set this back where you got it, and if I get bad off, don't you tell it." And I set it back just like he told me to, shut the door, and never did tell it.

No, he didn't get no sicker. He commenced gettin' better! He said, "Now, if it kills me, don't you never tell that you give it to me."

They never did miss the bread. They didn't say nothing about it, and I never did tell it.

OLLIE HALL, 1896
Stokes County

Malaria

Malaria
has been a scourge
for untold generations.
This was just accepted
as a way of life.

My father
would put a certain amount
of quinine
down on a white clean piece of paper
and take that capsule
and just chop it down on the paper
until it was full.

I remember
seeing him fill those capsules
as a child.

Bitter, very bitter!

LOUISE V. BOONE, 1922
Hertford County

Fear of a Bear

Old folks used to have to go to the salt lick in the fall to get their salt to salt down their meat with in the winter, you know. And my great-grandfather, he went to the salt lick and carried two horses with him. And the way they fixed to carry the salt, they filled up sacks with leaves or hay one, to put on the horses and tied them sacks down to keep that salt from hurting the horses' backs.

Well, he left to go to the salt lick to get the salt for the winter, and Grandma, she was left at the log cabin with no door to shut—they didn't say nothing about the windows, 'course I know they didn't have no windows—but she had no door to shut.

And one evening, between sundown and dark, she seen a bear coming down the ridge, or down the hill, and it came on over by the house and came to the hogpen and got the pig.

Well, they said that he threw off the top railings of the hogpen, you know, and he got that pig up in his foregrip, came right out of that pen and went over the ridge. Well, I've seen where the house was. I can remember my mother showing me where her grandfather lived.

Well, he went over the ridge and eat all he could out of it and put it over beside a log and covered it up with leaves.

But, poor old Grandma, she was scared so bad, right there with them three little boys, and she went and got an old mare and hitched her head in that door.

And Grandma set up all night and burned yarn rags. Scared so bad, and people lived so far apart, you know, afraid to start out with the children there at night. So she just set up and kept that old mare's head in the door and kept rags a-burnin' to keep the bear away.

No, they didn't have a door to close. Hadn't got that built yet.

MARTHA TOLIVER ABSHER, 1878
Alleghany County

Wild Boars

Now, right out here,
across from what they call
Barden's Cut,
was one
    of
      the
        most
          isolated
            little strands you
have ever seen in all your life. There were wild boars. Now, that used to be Diamond City. O. K. People lived out there and it was a whaling village. This was back in the late 1800s. Of course, they went way out to do their whaling, and they got pretty good-sized whales.

This little community they called Diamond City was only about a foot or two above high tide; it's even worse now. Real marshy, too. But people lived out there. However, storms started making little cuts through there, so that they couldn't stay. But those people had an ingenuity all their own; they could take two or three skiffs and move a house. So they jacked them up and rolled them down on logs and got them on skiffs and moved them over to Harkers Island. And that's when Harkers Island became settled—because they had to abandon Diamond City.

I've been over to Diamond City myself—what's left of it. Of course, they couldn't move their dead, and today you can see human skeletons. I found two or three skulls and a couple of leg bones, and a few things like that where gradually erosion would wash away the surface soil.

I remember one day I decided to go over there hunting, and I got the little old boat and pushed out across Barden's Cut. I went on around back of the island there. The marsh grass was up about this high, and all through there are these little cuts. I had on my hip boots, and I had my little old single-gauge shotgun. Sixteen-gauge, which is not too powerful, but I figured I'd conceal myself in the marsh grass, find me a little knoll there, and when a duck came by—flew by there—I'd raise up and kill me a duck.

So I finally found my spot, I guess about a mile from the lighthouse. And it was cold—oh, it was bitter cold! And there was no shelter from the wind. And I was just sitting there about to freeze, and I could see my skiff off out there about thirty feet or so. And all of a sudden I heard this noise behind me, and I raised up. It sounded like a herd of horses running or something. Now there was this little creek thing about three feet wide, and another little knoll over there. And there were these three wild hogs—boars. They had those curved, hooked tusks.

Now, what it was, when those people had to abandon Diamond City, they just had to leave their hogs. The hogs ran loose, and what they couldn't catch, they just left. So they became just like these old piney-woods rooters; they just degenerated and interbred with wild pigs and that's what I encountered that day. I was never so frightened in all my life. Now, I had my shotgun, but if I had shot one close range, the others would have charged me. And if I had wounded him—why, I would have never survived! There were three of them. They would have cut me to pieces.

So I just raised up and took about three steps and hit that water. In the meantime, the tide had started coming in, but I just waded right on out up above my boots and finally I got in my skiff. And they stood right there on the bank and watched me. I don't know if they could swim or not.

As I remember, and I didn't stand there and take too good notice, they must have stood about twenty-four or twenty-five inches high at the shoulders. They had a long snout, and they were big in the shoulders and small in the back. Why, I'll bet one of those hams wouldn't weigh over seven or eight pounds. They would be too strong to eat, however, because they eat fish scraps and all kinds of things.

Boy!

was I glad

to get home

that day!

JOHN D. COBLE, 1912
*Former lighthouse keeper, Cape Lookout,
now living in Stokes County*

Storms

I remember the storm in '33. It was a rough toime. It shore was. The house that I was in at that toime, the water came four feet deep in it. It moved the house a little, but it didn't tear it up.

There wasn't anybody lost in this section, but at the place, South River, which goes by the post office of Merrimon, there was noine lost. It was a hurricane. As far back as there is history there has been hurricanes through this section at toimes.

When I was young, the heat, the way we had at that toime was with wood burned in a wood stove. The way we cooked was with wood. And the ladies sure fared bad cookin' in the kitchen in the summertoime with a hot stove goin'. I can well remember.

And the people at that toime were fishermen. They got up before daylight and worked until after dark.

If you'd lived down here with us, back before World War II, if you used it, you either caught it or you had it in your field. You didn't go nowhere and buy it. Everybody always salted fish and had fish in the wintertoime. And anything else they used—growed cotton and carded it.

During the war there was a lot of sinking off the coast here. I saw the subs, and they'd sometoime come in roight close. I was goin' to sea at that toime. We'd see them at noight, and we knowed what they was.

CAPTAIN FLOYD DANIELS *of* The Pamlico
ferry between Cedar Island and Ocracoke, 1920
Carteret County

Hurricane

But that night, the wind got up to a hundred and thirty-five knots.

I couldn't stand up in the wind. I had to crawl from one building to the other. The water was sloshing around, you know. The last time I read it, the wind was a hundred and thirty-five knots, and that would be about a hundred and fifty-five or sixty miles per hour. It blew off some shingles, but it didn't get the roof. Those buildings are built for that kind of weather. And it's rough on the ships. I know. I've been in it.

But anyway, I got this reading, and I came back to my office, my little room, and I made my report by radio. My land line was out. So I went back the next hour to do the next one, and I turned the wind instrument to read the wind, and I couldn't get any reading. So, my goodness! Well, I couldn't do anything about it. It was up on top of a three-story building. Well, to make a long story short, about three days later, we found it about three hundred feet over on the side of a sand dune.

It was an anemometer, one of those three-cup spinning devices. It was gone, but we had to estimate what the wind was then. We'd been trained to do that. But it didn't get much higher. That was just about the maximum velocity.

The worst part lasted about four hours, but we felt the effects a lot longer. The seas were rough for a while. Worst of all was that we were just about out of supplies. We didn't have any groceries. They had to send supplies over from the mainland, and we didn't think we were going to get any. It was almost a week, as I remember. The Coast Guard was nearby, and they shared with us; but they didn't have much either. So we scrounged around and made out till the end of the month. The inland waters were rough, too, and a lot of new cuts had come across the beach.

JOHN D. COBLE, 1912
Former lighthouse keeper, Cape Lookout,
now living in Stokes County

8 SCHOOL AND CHURCH

Providing a welcome change from the routine of everyday life, school and church were highly esteemed in earlier days. Their unassuming structures did not prevent them from becoming impressive edifices in memory. Affectionate recollections center around an eccentric schoolmaster or a beloved preacher, and youthful antics are always recounted with a chuckle.

One-Teacher School

I went to a one-teacher school
back in the early 1900s.
That one teacher taught
me from the first grade
to about the eighth or ninth grade.
And we sat on a plank
with pegs under it for legs,
and when we got ready to do our writing,
we got on our knees
and used that for a desk.
Just sat on the bench most of the time
and held our books in our laps.

She was one of the finest teachers I ever saw.
She had discipline.
She had a leather strap about this long
and she cut it up into fingers.
About eight or ten fingers.
And she'd take you and hold your hand out there,
right before all of 'em,
and she'd just pop you with that thing.
And,
if you were too bad,
she'd use it on your behind, too.

They had discipline in those days.

HUBERT C. WOODALL, 1892
Johnston County

Preacher Hayes

There was Preacher Hayes.
He'd never been married,
and he wore a derby,
and he slept a lot,
and he chewed tobacco,
and he had a spittoon.

Well,
he was the teacher.
And one day
they moved the spittoon
and put his derby down there,
and he woke up.

After a while
he found out
he had spit his hat full.

MAGGIE JEFFERS, 1894
ETHEL LUTZ, 1898
BERTHA NORMAN, 1911
Cleveland County

Our Seats

Well, my first days in school was a little log cabin, oh, I suppose about twenty-five by thirty or something like that. And it was just heavy board floors, sawed out and put down. And our seats were slabs. Now, when they're sawing trees, you know, they saw off the outer bark, and there's kind of a slab with it. And they'd bore holes in that and put legs in them, and that's what we had to set on. That was our seats. We had no back.

No, they didn't smooth 'em down. They were plenty rough.

And our recreation, at mealtime, the boys would get out and play leapfrog, and the girls would march. And we would play Ring around the Rosey. And we'd sing this song: "Reading and writing and 'rithmetic; march to the tune of the hickory stick!" And, of course, the boys played ball, too.

We carried our lunches with us, and we walked about two miles each way. No, we didn't cross a bridge—we crossed a footlog. The creek wasn't very deep, and there was a footlog put across the stream. And we went across on that. There was a handrail that we could hold onto and get across in the wintertime. It could be rough in the wintertime. Especially when it was icy and raining a little bit.

NORA C. WAGONER, 1882
Alleghany County

Dinner Buckets

Children back then
carried their lunches to school
in baskets or lard buckets.

They had pies and corn bread and molasses
and sweet 'taters, Irish 'taters.

Well, you didn't have light bread
Unless your mama made the light bread.
You'd have big old biscuits.
Potatoes.
Molasses. Put 'em in a little jar.
Have 'em with cornbread.

Law, children don't know nothing now.

Put molasses in the teacher's coat pocket.

They'd have a cloakroom,
and they had benches in there.
They'd hang their coats up and
the benches to set their dinner on.

And the children were always gettin'
into other people's dinner buckets.

BERTHA NORMAN, 1911
Burke County

Days of the Blue Back Speller

We used to go to subscription schools, and my pappy would pay for me. Seems like it was sometimes a dollar a month. You know, money meant a whole lot more then.

I remember it was just a little bit of a log cabin, and you could stick your fingers down through the cracks in the floor.

There was one single row of windows by the workbench. That was all the light we had, don't you know. But they were all broken out and it was open through there. The bottom of the door was worn away, too. And that was our school.

We went just three months during the cold wintertime. We had a big old fireplace, and the teacher and children would go out to the woods and bring in brush to make a fire. Then there was a spring right near there. If we wanted a drink of water, we went to the spring. But sometimes little old mean schoolboys would run down and muddy the spring before we could get to it. Made us so mad! But that's what they'd do; they'd muddy the spring. We couldn't hardly get a decent drink of water.

We had six lessons a day: Blue Back spelling, arithmetic, readers—we commenced at first reader and went on through the fifth, all through school, don't you know. The little ones read in the first reader, and the bigger ones read on up in the others.

Then we had history and geography, and . . . I can't remember what the other one was called. It was when they asked you all kinds of questions about things. Grammar? I guess that's what it was—grammar.

And we had dictionary and blackboard writing with arithmetic. Of course, we used slates. Every night we had spelling—and dictionary. If we stood the head of our school three nights we got a "Head Mark." We always broke up at four o'clock, and the "night lesson" was the last lesson of the day, and it was spelling.

For geography, we sang all the states and their capitals and rivers. The teacher had us to sing, and it was pretty! [Grandma Spencer began tapping her fingers on the arm of her chair and singing in her best Primitive Baptist form.]

"New Hampshire, Concord, on the Merrimack River. . ." [repeated three or four times, then on to the next state] "Rhode Island has two capitals: Providence and Newport . . ." You know they've put them together now, and they've just got one. "Massachusetts, Boston, on the Boston harbor. . . ." [song ended].

Come on down, you get to West Virginia. We had forty-four states then. You know, we've got more than that now.

That was our first school. For our next school, our daddies went out in the woods and cut the logs and built this schoolhouse out here. Now it's been made into a house, but then it was a schoolhouse. And it was a pretty good one, tight and warm, with windows in both ends. We didn't have school the year they were building the schoolhouse. And I went there three years. Our schoolmaster was Reverend Ashburn. He boarded over near North View Church, about four or five miles away at Wes Morefield's; and he walked over to school every day. Once a week he broke the ice in the creek and took a cold bath.

MINNIE LEE SPENCER, 1879
Stokes County

Children's Pranks

Teachers,
they would either
walk or drive a buggy
or ride a horse.

And they'd sometimes tie
their horse up behind the schoolhouse.
And a lot of mean children
would go turn their buggy over.

And the mean boys and girls
would do things like
putting animals and things
in the teacher's desk,
and wouldn't nobody tell on the other one.

We'd go out and maybe find
an old crow or buzzard or something,
just for, you know, meanness.
And mean boys would put shot in the stove
and it would blow the lids off.
It'd nearly scare her to death,
and they just wouldn't tell on each
other and she'd have to keep
the whole class in.

BERTHA NORMAN, 1911
Burke County

Discipline at Creason

We had a school down here at Creason, and they were anywhere from six to twenty-eight years old in there. The big ones had something like a bookkeeper's desk up about this high. And we set on benches without any backs to 'em. The only time we sat up correctly was when the fellow behind us would have a pin stuck in the end of his shoe and let us have it in the back end.

And there were paper spitballs all over the ceiling and a big old stove in the middle with a chimney. We had windows just on one side. It was the west side in this case. Had a teacher with one half of her face gone to a birthmark, but she was a very sweet person. Miss Nannie Watson.

The discipline? Why, it was all right. We got out there and fought once in a while. One feller tried to sick litt'ole Jim on me one time. I didn't know what it was all about, but he got me excited, and I must of hit him harder than I thought I did because he didn't come to school for several days. I had cut a big hole here and another one up here [demonstrates].

He claimed I'd done it with knucks or a railroad tap, but it was just that he had me excited, and I hit him harder than I thought I had. Never nothing come of it. He got all right.

    I still don't know what he was mad at me about. He just come at me.

LEE EDWIN KISER, D.C., 1898
Iredell County, speaking of his boyhood in Stokes

Outdoor Facilities

Whenever we had a play
down here at Creason School,
we had to improvise a stage
on the outside of the building.

We would build the platform
and enclose it with pine or cedar boughs.

And yet the children today
fuss about
"inadequate equipment."

We didn't even have a spring. . . .

There weren't no toilets.

The girls would go one direction,
the boys, another.

In the woods.

LEE EDWIN KISER, D.C., 1898
Iredell County, speaking of his boyhood in Stokes

Walking to Church

We usually went to church on Sunday.

It was three miles to church
from Air Bellows.

And usually we walked to church.

We had Sunday shoes,
but we didn't wear them on the way to church.

We'd walk barefooted until
we got on up to about
half a mile of church,
then we'd stop and sit down
and put on our shoes and stockings.

Osborne

And then we went on to church.

Well, we usually had company
going back home
so we didn't take our shoes off going back.

NORA C. WAGONER, 1882
Alleghany County

Aprons and Overalls

My mother
would wear aprons
to church.
And we starched
all our clothes.
Pillowcases—just everything we starched.
And women would wear
aprons and bonnets
to church at that time,
and men
would wear overalls.

Go in the wagon.
And if it was cold,
my daddy

has heated brick
and put in the wagon
to try to keep
our feet warm.
Wrapped 'em in old tow sacks.

ETHEL LUTZ, 1898
Cleveland County

Preaching Once a Month

People
went to four or five churches.

Didn't have preaching but
once a month.
Methodist.
Missionary Baptist.
Free Will Bap—Oh, I don't know—all of 'em.

But one of 'em preached
first Sunday,
'nother one of 'em second Sunday—
just have preachin' at your church once a month.

But
everybody went around to
all the other churches.

I've heard 'em talk about
goin' to all four churches every month.

HUBERT C. WOODALL, 1892
Johnston County

Brush Arbor

They had a brush arbor
right out there where my house is now.

And they had benches of slabs
in there to set on.

And they had pine brush
over the top of it
to keep the sun out of it.

Just had poles all around to hold
the top up.
And we went out there lots of times
to that old camp meetin'.

Brush arbor.

Then they tore that down
and built just a small church.

And then they tore that down
and built 'em a big church.

ETHEL LUTZ, 1898
Cleveland County

The Pounding

And we didn't have a baptismal place in the church. We had to go to a pond to be baptised. They were usually made from a spring.

We had prayer meeting, and we'd go out in the grove. They'd all come together and when they needed rain, they'd pray for rain. They were more in earnest then. They were.

And you could hear the preacher a mile away. And I mean they *preached*!

And we used to give the preachers a lot, you know, instead of paying 'em a big salary. Everyone tried to give 'em something. We'd have what we called a pounding and take all kinds of things for 'em. Food and clothing, too. We didn't have a whole lot of money to give.

A dollar was a dollar in that day and time. And we worked for 'em. Why, I picked a many a gallon of blackberries for ten cents a gallon. Now, that's how we worked. And we were so glad to get it. When I was a little girl, going around barefooted, I'd pick ten gallons of blackberries a day.

CLEO ELAM, 1902
Cleveland County

Primitive Baptist Preaching

Since there weren't any newspapers or any books to speak of back then, there wasn't much entertainment except maybe to go to mill and talk with others there or maybe go to preaching when they were having the quarterly meeting or the annual meeting or monthly meeting.

There weren't enough preachers to go around, and so sometimes at a certain church there would be preaching only twice a month.

In fact, among the Primitive Baptists, who are the direct descendants of the old Baptists in the colonial period and in many respects have not changed either their faith or their practice from the time before the Revolutionary War, these meetings were the big social occasions for the rural farm families.

Some of those old Primitive Baptist preachers used to come down this way to preach. One of them was an old Elder Marshall. I've forgotten what his first name was, but he was tongue-tied. He stuttered terribly.

Now, some of those preachers had limited gifts, very limited. But others were really gifted. They could strike that Welsh chant. It really came out of the Welsh Baptist that was so dominant in the formation of the Baptist faith in Pennsylvania and which was more or less brought into this area by the preachers from the Philadelphia Association who came through here in 1745, '55, '65, along through there. And it sort of took hold, and some preachers started using that type of preaching.

And Elder Denny, my grandmother's preacher, was one of the best I ever heard. He could read his scripture, warm up to his subject, and then he could just go in musical, rhythmical verse, and he could just carry people along with him. And he was not a college man, but he was well read and self-educated, and he could preach in a way that would be acceptable to anybody.

But, instead of the repetition that some of the less-gifted ones had, he just kept on and on.

New pictures. He was a "type and shadow" preacher. He picked out the types in the Old Testament and showed how they threw a shadow of things to come, and how the New Testament fulfilled the Old Testament; and, of course, he applied it to people today. And he was just wonderful at that.

But old Elder Marshall, I've heard him a number of times. And, talking like we're talking, he'd stutter terribly. He'd been like that all his life.

He'd get up and read his text slowly. He'd speak slowly and a little haltingly, and after he warmed up to it, he just poured out the gospel without a hesitation.

When he was just a boy, after he was converted to the Baptist faith up in the county-line area, he felt this impulse to preach. And he said, "Lord, I can't preach. I can't go before a church and ask to be tried." Yes, he was a stutterer from his youth, even as a child. And so finally the impression within him was so strong that he went before the church and asked if they would liberate him to say a few words.

Now, when anybody is liberated to preach like that, he doesn't go up in the pulpit. He just goes up in front of the church to exercise his gifts, if he has any. And they decide if he has a gift, and they will later ordain him, and he can go up in the pulpit. But at that point, you're down in the floor just exercising your gifts.

Well, he proved to them he was called, and when he got wound up, he could preach. So he was ordained, and at eighty, eighty-one years old, the old gentleman was still serving his God. It was really an inspiration to know and hear a man like that.

HUGH B. JOHNSTON, JR., 1913
Wilson County

To Church in a Wagon

When we were
growing up
at my pappy's house,
we always went to church
in the wagon.
And we didn't just go to one church;
we went all around
to different churches.
We'd start out
and go down the road,
and there would be somebody

standing down by their gate.
And we'd stop and
pick them up
and take them with us.

People were always
waiting along the way,
and we just
picked them up.

We loved to have them.

MINNIE LEE SPENCER, 1879
Stokes County

The 'Sociation

We used to have camp meetin's.
My father never did join the
Primitive Baptist Church. That was
the old church.
But he had the preacher that would
come down from—
he drove down thirty miles—
come down here to preach.
Preached on Saturday and Sunday.

And then they had the 'Sociation.
That was a two-day meetin'.
They didn't camp, but I've seen
my father sleep as many as fifteen and
twenty in his house.
He just spread 'em on the floor.
Just let 'em sleep on the floor.
Just sleep 'em and feed 'em.
And they had all kinds of food.
Just killed big hogs and barbecued hams.
And when they'd go to the 'Sociations,
everybody carried food.
And they don't have those kind of
things anymore.

HUBERT C. WOODALL, 1892
Johnston County

Singing in Church

This is the old Primitive Baptist hymnbook, published in 1924. I have two or three around here that are older than that. This is common meter, "C. M.," and "L. M." is long meter. And so they're all in here. Watts's hymns. It's a collection, naturally, that the Primitive Baptists approved of. And if they didn't approve of a hymn, it didn't get into the hymnbook.

My grandma's favorite hymn is "Amazing Grace." Now, I can remember a few old ladies and gentlemen who did their best to sing, but they didn't have any ear, and they'd sing off key. I remember one old lady who had a high-pitched voice, and you could hear her above everybody else. That was one of the things you accepted. Some people don't hear, and they can't tell when they are off.

In some of the churches there were people who were rather gifted, and here and there was somebody who could sing tenor. And usually somebody just heisted the tune, and then they all sang together as best they could. But in some of the churches there would be somebody who could add tenor, or maybe bass or alto, and I have heard really very harmonious singing at times.

But, again, out in the rural churches, there would often be some old gentleman or lady who wanted to sing and didn't have any talent. So you'd hear some of the most amazing discordances.

But the idea, the purpose, was to sing together.

HUGH B. JOHNSTON, JR., 1913
Wilson County

Proselyting

There were two Presbyterian preachers that went up here in the mountains, proselyting or finding out what they could do to spread the Presbyterian church up in there. 'Course, they didn't have anything but Baptists and Methodists.

And they went up to this house, and they asked this woman, says, "Are there any Presbyterians up here?"

She said, "I don't know, but Pa killed some kind of a varmint the other night, and skun it, and its hide is tacked up down there on the crib door. You can go and see if that's what it is."

I happen to know who one of the preachers was, too. Sure, that really happened. It was old Mr. Miller, the pious, fine old Presbyterian minister from down in Woodleaf.

But this was when he was a young man. And old Mr. Brown, who was pastor of the Presbyterian church down in Barium Springs, was with him. They were up in the mountains taking a survey. And this woman just didn't know what a Presbyterian was.

LOUISE PHILLIPS KISER, 1898
Iredell County

9 SOCIAL CUSTOMS

These were the days of the fan and the watch fob. As head of the family, the image of the male was respected—at times, even revered—while woman filled her indispensable role in the home and the field. Among younger folk, courting was a gratifying departure from the tedium of workaday life, and the whole neighborhood took delight in looking on. Social ethics were staunch, honesty and integrity ruled, and often the most valued thing a man had to offer was his word. Around the institution of the country store revolved a social order all its own. Meanwhile, barn dances and mineral-water spas in the state attracted ardent followers.

A Man's World

Now,
let me tell you something:

When I grew up,
just about
all the men who got letters
had that
"Esquire"
after their names.

I
don't know why.

But
that was
a man's world back then!

MINNIE E. MOORE, 1884
Forsyth County

Courting

When it come to courtin',
you had a horse and buggy,
and that's all you had.

We were fortunate.
We had two horses.
We had a stable out in back,
and we had a surrey.
We could use one horse or two horses.
Use a tongue or use a shaft.

And I remember, one time
we were out in the country courtin'—
me and my girl—she later became my wife.

We were out on a country road somewhere.
And a man went back and told everybody—
he passed us—
said we'd tied our lines around the buggy whip,
and we was doin' our courtin' just ridin' along.

HUBERT C. WOODALL, 1892
Johnston County

The Parlor

And a lot of people walked five or six miles
to go to see their girl. Didn't have any transportation. Had to start out pretty early. Take you about
an hour to walk four miles. 'Course, you had to be
up in your teens.

You know, everybody had a parlor. And the
old folks sat in the bedroom. And that parlor was
kept just as clean and dark, you know. They didn't
never open the windows on 'em much. And you
did your courtin' there.

My folks never did set around much, and
not many of 'em did. Most of 'em would go on and
turn the parlor over to the young folks.

No, we didn't take no flowers. Oh,
sometimes we might cut some out of our yard and
take 'em. There wasn't no such thing as a florist in
those days. I 'member when I used to—we'd
always carry our girls some candy. Box of candy.
Things of that kind. And I'd carry my girl some
flowers now and then that I cut out of the yard.

But I think people enjoyed living back then
as much as they do today. But it was just a
different kind of living. I know I did; I enjoyed my
young days. As I said, I was married before I ever
rode in an automobile.

HUBERT C. WOODALL, 1892
Johnston County

Dating Customs

Oh,
our courtin' was altogether different.
A boy hardly ever kissed a girl
without they was gettin' pretty far along.
If you saw a—
you know,
they wore long dresses.
I never saw my first wife
above her shoe tops
till after we was married.
If you went to see a girl
over three or four times,
why,
it was gettin' pretty far along.
If you didn't keep slippin' around,
people would begin to talk.

Now'n,
a boy can date a girl here,
then go over yonder fifty miles
and date another one,
and she don't know anything about it.

The whole neighborhood knew about it then.

CARME ELAM, 1896
Cleveland County

Daddy Looks On

All
we
did
was go in the living room,
in the parlor,
they called it then.
And sit there and talk.

And somebody was always watching us
around the corner.
My daddy.
And then he'd call "Bedtime!" on us.

I was scared to death
to let a boy kiss me back then
because I knew
my daddy would slap my jaws.

Well,
he never did slap my jaws,
but
he was particular with me.

MAGGIE JEFFERS, 1894
ETHEL LUTZ, 1898
Cleveland County

Closer

They told it
on me.
'Course, it wadn't so.

I wouldn't a done
a thing like that:
I
had
a
horse,
and its name was "Closer."
And I'd say,
"Come up, Closer!"
And my girl
thought I was talkin' to her,
and she'd slide over.

I
had to talk
to Closer
a whole lot, too.

Yeah.
You had to work your head.

CARME ELAM, 1896
Cleveland County

The Suitor

A young man would sometimes pick out a family, a certain family, that he wanted to marry into. And he'd start out with the oldest one. And she'd get sick of him and get another boyfriend. And he'd go to the next one.

And, if you'd pay any attention to him atall, he'd come. He never made a date. Never known to make a date. But he'd come out—and this boy that we had, this boyfriend that we had, he'd come with a box—he worked for a florist, and he'd come out with a box this long of long-stemmed roses or carnations. Mostly carnations.

And my father couldn't stand to smell carnations overnight in a room, shut up in a room. "Whew! Get that out of here!" and he'd mention the boy's name—"[So and so's] been here." He knew he had, you know.

But he'd come with an armful, or a box of candy, or something like that. Just *very*, too nice, just too nice. Dressed in his Sunday best.

And the next one in line would try to entertain him and set and talk about nothing or go for a walk, an afternoon walk, you know, in the summertime. And then she couldn't stand it any longer. She'd get another beau or go somewhere and be gone because he did not make a date. So you didn't know if he was coming or not. And we'd try to get away from home before he got there. So he'd come out, and maybe the next one would be there. He went on down to the baby. And the last time he came, why, she got her hat . . . said, "I'm going with you" whenever the next one started out, and left him there with his beautiful bouquet of flowers. And, finally, he quit coming after—I guess he came probably a half dozen times after that and there was really nobody. He'd just come with his armful of flowers. And he finally went away, went out west. How did he get to our house? Walked. All the way from Asheville. Five miles. Walked five miles out there in rain or shine.

And his flowers—why, they were beautiful ones. They'd last for a week. I loved the flowers. I think maybe they were the ones that were supposed to have been sold yesterday, the ones that were left over from Saturday.

FRANCES C. COLE, 1890
Buncombe County

The Family Name

Your ancestors
meant much more to you
than they do now.

You don't think
what kind of a family
your daughter
is marrying into now.

Nothing like
it used to be.
I know that was one thing
people were particular about.

And my mother would say,
"Very nice young man,
but I don't like his name."

And then
another would say,
"Well,
he's not
Scotch."

MARY C. MC KINNON, 1886
Scotland County

Fashions

Oh, yes. We wore long dresses. They almost touched the floor. Your slippers showed beneath your dress. Real full skirts. Tiny waists. I had a twenty-inch waist. I remember one that was especially pretty had a round neck and came off the shoulders and had a little strap here.

And we wore slippers. 'Course, we didn't dare show our stocking—oh, that wasn't nice atall. You wore your dress to cover your leg. You didn't even show your ankle. And I wore a size 3½ shoe then. And I wear a 7½ now, but I think they've changed the sizes.

But we wore big hats. You ought to have seen my hats. Wide brims, with great big flowers on the front of them. Always loved hats.

And always carried a parasol. Your parasol was your most expensive apparel because you had to pay a dollar for a nice parasol then. We did have some cheaper than that, but I imagine they were pretty cheap.

But our parasols then had ruffles around the edge of them. They were very pretty. They were for the sun. You used them in the sun. Oh, you didn't dare get a freckle or tan. Oh, a tanned girl would have been awful at that time! Just the whiter and the pinker you could be. And the only kind of makeup we wore was powder, already done up. You would buy it sewed up in a little bag, and you done thisaway [demonstrates]. And you didn't use lipstick. There was no such thing as lipstick then. We'd pinch our cheeks to make 'em rosy. Or we had artificial roses that were red. 'Course, it was dye. Dyed to make it red. Because if you got in the rain, you'd have red stuff all over you. It'd run down. And you'd take one of those rose petals and wet it and paint your cheeks with it. I didn't use them much.

FRANCES C. COLE, 1890
Buncombe County

The Fan

But we also carried a fan.
Always a fan.
To cool off when you'd go to church
or Sunday school.
Why,
very gracefully,
you used your fan.
'Course,
if anybody looked at you too cute
or smiled too much,

you could put your fan up
so that they couldn't see you.
Then you'd lower your fan
a little
and look over it
to see if they were still looking at you.
Oh, yes, the fans!
And such pretty ones!
The fans cost more than the parasols.

Beautiful.

FRANCES C. COLE, 1890
Buncombe County

Watch Fobs and Removable Collars

Usually a man wore a watch fob with a ribbon like a decoration, and it could have various emblems on it. Now, a watch fob would hang down off the watch, and the watch pocket was over here on your right-hand side, just above the waist. You could just take a hold of it and pull your watch out. It hung down by a link or two of chain. And then, you might have a chain on the watch, too. Pocket watch.

Oh, yes, we used to wear those removable collars on shirts all the time. Wear 'em real high, and I've slept in 'em. I don't know how, but I did. Oh, and just as stiff. Just like an oxen gettin' used to a yoke.

They were hard, and they fastened to the collar by buttons. They had a hole back here in the back and one up in the front. The front one was thicker because you only put one thickness of the collar on in the back. See, your shirt didn't have any collar. And then you brought it around here, and you had two thicknesses.

They made those collars stiff with starch. Just starch 'em real stiff and iron 'em. And it took a long time to get 'em dry.

'Course, people who wanted to get by cheap would have celluloid collars. A few, but that was not dressed up, now. 1913, along there.

LEE EDWIN KISER, D.C., 1898
Iredell County

Trips into Town

You'd come to town occasionally. We were seven miles from Murfreesboro, and we'd come to town, maybe every, oh, I don't know, a few times a year. But we had country stores we could go to for the necessities. So we didn't have to come to a village like Murfreesboro so often because we could go to these stores and pick up—we'd carry chickens and eggs, meat, and trade for the things that we needed. We didn't have to have but very little money.

Now, the men would go to the store on a day when it was rainy, or something like that, that they couldn't work in the field. Why, they would gather at the store. And they would really have a lot of fun just visiting with each other.

Well, they'd have the staples that we'd need at the country store. And they would carry some dry goods, they would call it, and some yard goods. And some shoes. They carried most of the things that you'd need for everyday living.

Kerosene. That was very important because that was the only means of lighting that we had in those days, was using kerosene in lamps and lanterns. And we had open fireplaces. And they served for the heat and light, too, in a good many cases because—unless they tried to read, they wouldn't have the—that is, you wouldn't spend that much money unnecessarily. You would do without it unless you were reading because you'd have enough light from the fireplace. Used that kerosene just when you really needed it.

Kerosene cost about ten or twelve cents a gallon. And that was a lot of money then. Expensive light.

Oh, yes, pickle barrels. Cracker barrels. Dogs would follow them to the store, but they'd stay on the outside.

Fact is, I had a country store myself, from the time I was fifteen years old. I was there eight years. We had a gathering place there. I have fond memories of it and the good times people had. Every night people would come in and stay, probably, till nine-thirty. Never any more than ten o'clock. Didn't stay out too late.

Now, the husband, he'd go to the store, not every night, but some nights. And the wife would visit some other neighbor. He'd take her by to the neighbor's house.

These country stores, they would be a place to trade their produce—chickens, eggs. They'd take out goods in exchange. They didn't have money. A dress length or several gallons of kerosene. A new axe head or an axe handle. Salt. Sugar. I remember very well going to the store with my mother in a horse and buggy and we'd always carry everything we needed to exchange for produce. We didn't need the money, actually.

That wasn't the important thing. The important
thing in those days was to grow produce enough
to exchange for the things you needed.

CHARLES L. REVELLE, SR., 1900
Hertford County

A Man's Word

Back in those early days
when I first went into business,
it was during the Depression.
And nobody had any money.

We all kindly had to depend on each other.
We would trade a lot.
People would come in;
and they would trade ham, butter, eggs,
or what-have-you
for the merchandise they had to have.

And the expression was—
you just can't believe it—
but the expression was
"My word's my bond."

And when a man gave me his word,
why, to me,
it was worth a stack of notes
a foot high.
because he meant just what he said.

"My word is my bond." I knew it was true.

R. HOLTON GENTRY, 1909
Stokes County

Drinking Mineral Water

And I've heard a lot of people say,
and they would swear by it,
that the Moore's Springs water was good to drink
and that it was good to bathe in.
And I think it was good.
I think it was wonderful;
I still enjoy drinking the water from Moore's
Springs.
And I'm still sold in my mind
that it is the most beneficial
to digestion
of anything that we could use.
I still have my five-gallon jug in the basement

where I used to go and get water
and bring it here and drink it, you know.

Yes, people had faith in it.
Really did.
And I think it did people a lot of good.
Yes, indeed,
they had an old hand pump there in the
springhouse. I've seen people backed up,
lined up there to get water.
You just couldn't believe that many people
would get over there
and stand in line to get some water to drink.

Now, they weren't necessarily "jugging" it;
they were just going to get a drink.
And, of course, some of 'em would express it,
"OOOOOeeee, that's *awful!*"
But, the ones of 'em that had drunk it before
and knew about it,
why, they were just crazy about it.

R. HOLTON GENTRY, 1909
Stokes County

Selling the Water

I remember
when they'd haul it
in oak barrels
all the way to Rural Hall
in oak barrels on a wagon.

Then, later on,
they got glass bottles.
And they would ship it,
six gallons to a case.
Half-gallon bottles.
And then they had big five-gallon demijohns.

Back in the 1880s, used to,
the cows on this side of the river
would shed off earlier in the spring
than the cows on the other side.

And they looked so much nicer and healthier.
But they wouldn't drink any water

except
that spring water.

They'd go right to it.

W. ROYCE MOORE, 1910
Forsyth County,
speaking of Moore's Springs in Stokes

Mountain Dances

Well, the old mountain people had lots of different songs. The old mountain fiddlers and old banjo pickers, they had a lot of different songs that they played and sung. And we'd go to dances. We'd have big dances, and they had many different songs. One of 'em was "Black-eyed Susie," and then another, "Golden Slippers," and "Sourwood Honey."

Now, the dancing, we called it the Old Virginia Reel. You could dance as many couples as you wanted to, as you had room to. If you had a big enough floor, you could dance a hundred if you wanted to.

They'd dance any place that was big enough. Lots of times just in the homes. They'd, maybe on Saturday night, oh, about four, five, six

girls and four, five, six boys just get 'em a fiddler and get 'em a banjo picker and say, "Well, we can have us a dance down at So-and-So's." And they'd gather up and come and stay till maybe twelve or one o'clock. Dance. Mess around.

REED HAWKINS, 1895
Buncombe County

The fellers might have a drink, but the girls didn't drink. The fellers would have white corn liquor, and get 'em a drink. Oh, they'd get awfully funny! Yeah, they'd dance—Oh! And then dance on out the door and down the—gettin' in such a way of dancing.

FRANCES C. COLE, 1890
Buncombe County

Now, when I built my barn up yonder, I give 'em a dance. Oh, gosh! That was a tremendous crowd. And that was a barn dance. Yeah, a barn dance. I put a floor in it, and made a upstairs. Made stalls downstairs and then put a floor in it upstairs.

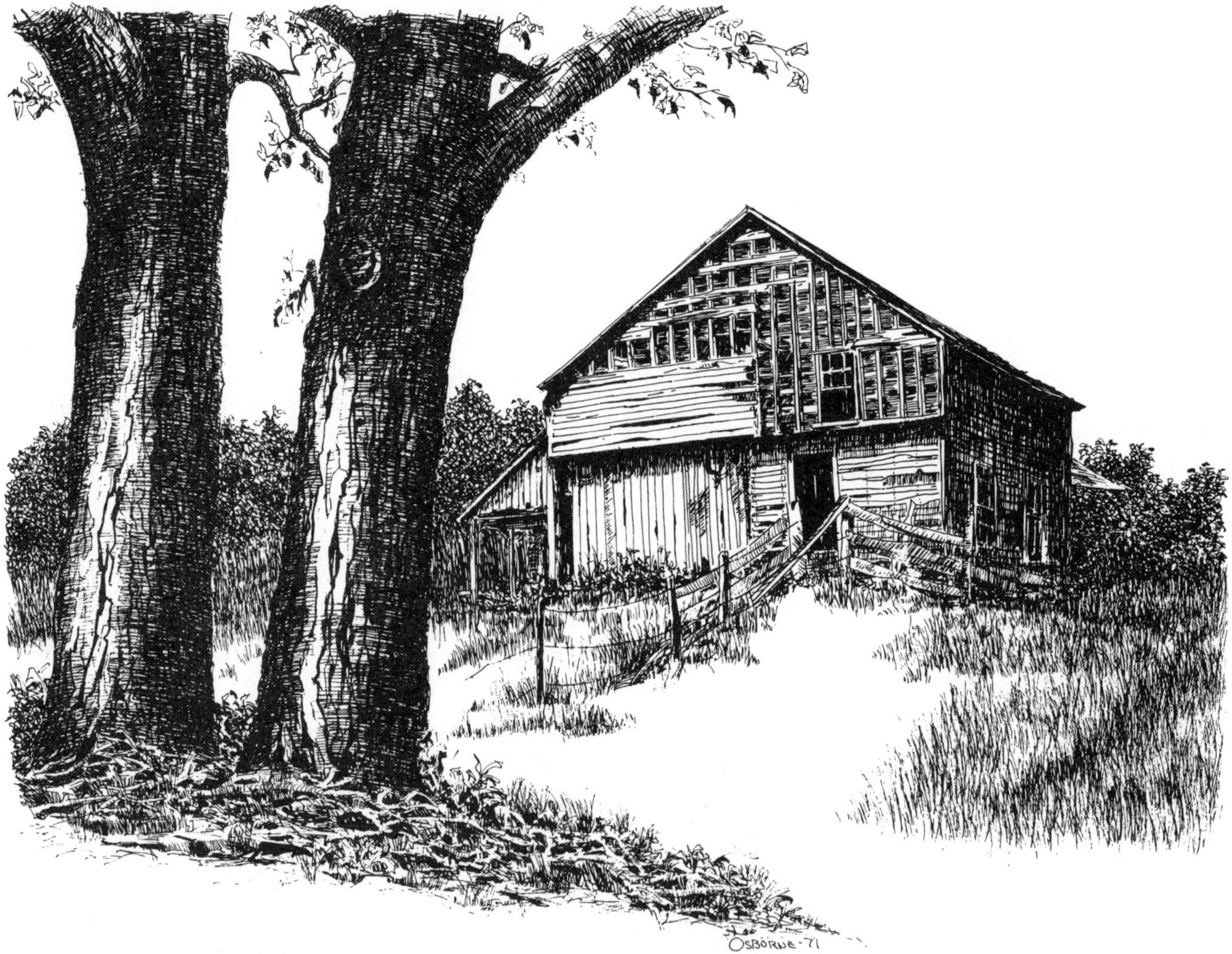
OSBORNE-71

And they wanted a dance. And I just says,
"Well, just go ahead, what you want." And I never
will forget, Lena, she was Odell's girl, and Stacey
and Bonnie. They come, but they said, "Now,
Grandpa will get us." But he didn't; he just
laughed about it.

REED HAWKINS, 1895
Buncombe County

The Fiddle and the Banjo

You see, a lot of people in the mountains,
back when I was a boy,
they was a lot of people thought
the devil was in a fiddle 'n' banjo.

That was back—way back.
And not all the people, but a great percent
thought the devil was in a fiddle 'n' banjo.
They wouldn't let you come in their home
with a banjo or a fiddle.

And I'll tell you
where it got its bad name.
A lot of people used to make blockade liquor,

and they'd get 'em a drank or two of liquor.
And they'd get happy.

And they'd go picking the banjo,
playing the fiddle, blowing the French harp.
And, the first thing you know, somebody
would get mad.
And somebody would throw a knife in somebody,
or somebody would shoot somebody.
Well, they thought
that if it hadn't been for the fiddle and the banjo,
it wouldn't a-happened.

Ain't that right?

That's right!

REED HAWKINS, 1895
Buncombe County

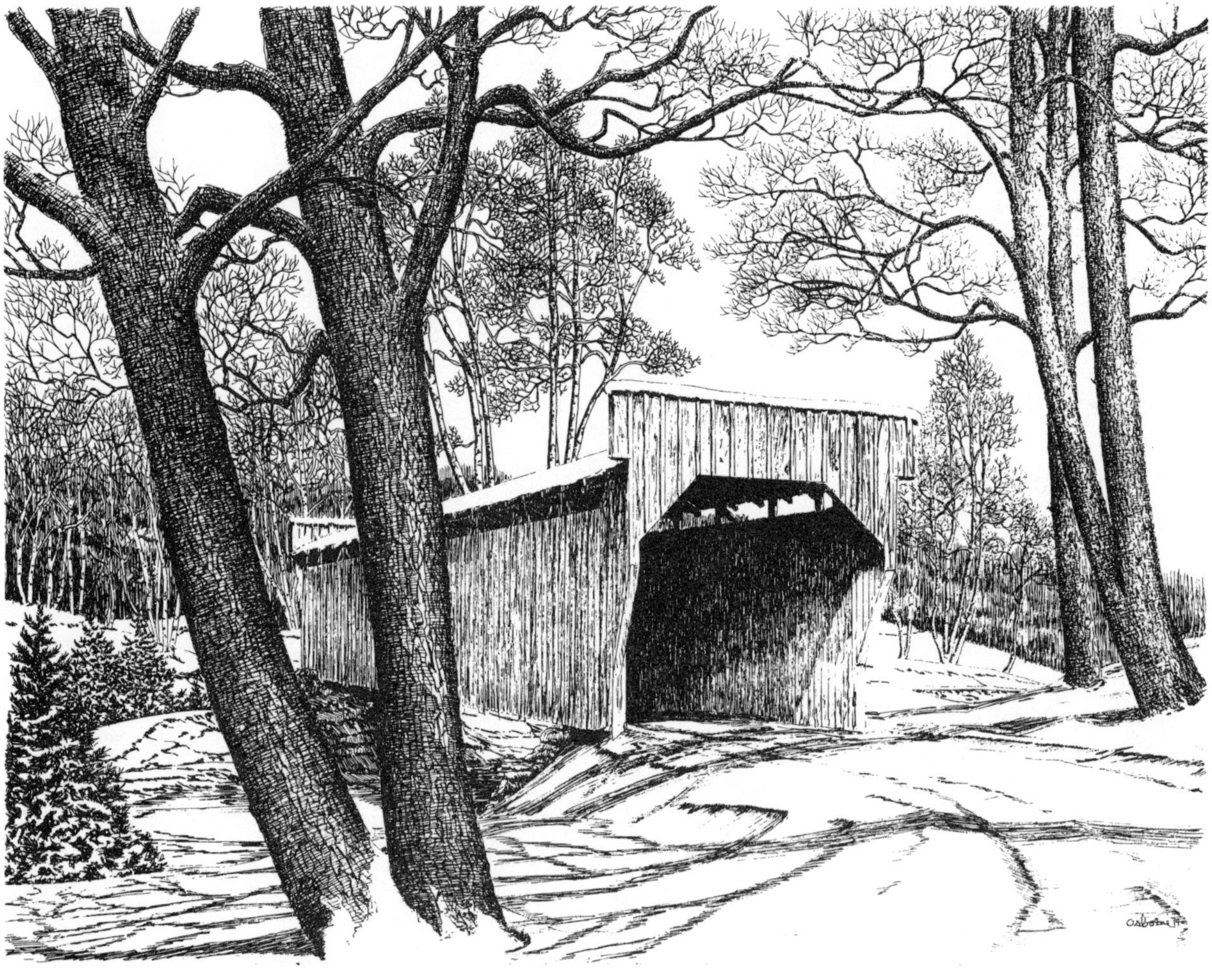

10 TRAVEL

People seldom traveled long distances. Schools, churches, country stores, and the homes of relatives were located rather near at hand. Covered bridges spanned the larger streams, and ferries appeared at crossing points. Popular footpaths were widened to accommodate horse and cart or wagon. As time passed, however, the advent of the buggy and the surrey called attention to the need for better roads. Labor for improvement was drafted from the local citizenry. Soon the countryside buzzed with the excitement of the first automobiles, and North Carolina was launched into the motor age.

Covered Bridges

We had a covered bridge across the Neuse River down here. Just beyond the river, we used to have a pasture. And we had to carry our cow to the pasture which was about a quarter of a mile, I reckon, but we'd take that cow and put her in the pasture every morning. That was my job. And my brother, he had to go get the cow in the evening. And bring that cow back in. And we had to take her across that bridge. It was a right long bridge. It got kindly dark in there. That bridge there was two hundred feet long, at least.

But all of your bridges was covered bridges then if there was any span to 'em, much. See, that was your support. You put a big pillar over here, and then you could go a hundred feet without puttin' any pillar. And then they were held up by the weight from above. They were what they called "tied together." And the coverin' and all give 'em support. Yeah. You see, the Neuse River and the lowlands made you have to have a right long bridge down here.

HUBERT C. WOODALL, 1892
Johnston County

Condition of the Roads

The old roads were just one continuous mudhole. There was nothing to make 'em out of but just red mud. I believe they called it "conscriptin'." They had an overseer.

He'd send word when they were going to work the road, and after you got seventeen or eighteen, you had to go to work a day or so on the road.

And right along in front of your house was one of the worst places there was, because the woods came close to the road. And it was a low place there. And the hollow went right down by the old packhouse. And that was a terrible place.

Why, the mudholes, you'd fall off two or three feet into 'em, and if you didn't have a pretty good team, you couldn't get out.

LEE EDWIN KISER, D.C., 1898
Iredell County

Conscription

We used to, I remember when every man had to work the roads, the highways, or hire somebody to work 'em for him if he was able to hire somebody, so many days a year.

Just got out there with shovels and carts and filled up holes. And just hauled—had what they called a dump cart and a mule or a horse. Course, they didn't have anything but horse and buggies and wagons in those days.

I 'member when there wasn't any paved road—well, the only paved road I ever remember way back yonder was going from here to Raleigh. Just as you come out of Raleigh, what they called "Hick's Hill."

About two miles they had a road about eight feet wide, and if you met a horse and buggy coming, each one of you had to get off, or just keep two wheels on enough to let the other one get by. That was kind of a cement road.

HUBERT C. WOODALL, 1892
Johnston County

Plank and Corduroy Roads

Since the roads were few in the old days and the farms were scattered, a person didn't necessarily want to take the time or the trouble to go all the way out to the main road, such as it was . . . to reach his neighbor's house.

And so, obviously, they had real little footpaths by which they could take shortcuts.

And where there were no large streams, only those that they could jump across—or maybe there would be an old log that they could walk across—why, the persons who were in a hurry could go from farm to farm along these paths.

Some of them were used for getting down in the woods to where they were gathering turpentine. Before the Civil War, around this area particularly, the gathering of turpentine was one of the main sources of cash income. There was a little cotton grown, and maybe a few stalks of tobacco here and there, but tobacco didn't come to Wilson County as a money crop until around 1890. That was the year the first market was held here.

Before the Civil War, in this area, seemingly, the pine forests were an almost inexhaustible source of tar and turpentine, which were commercially used for paints. And the tar itself was very valuable as a naval store in the days of the wooden vessels. Things to do with the building and keeping up of ships.

Now, during that period, at least before 1840, there was no railroad through here, and the only convenient way to get saleable items out was to load them in carts and haul them to the nearest landing.

Now, in Wilson County, Contentnea Creek passes through Stantonsburg and goes on up. About ten miles west of Wilson it changes its name and is known as Moccasin Creek. Well, the falls line in Wilson County is approximately where 301 South crosses Contentnea Creek. Now, the falls line is where the streams of the coastal plain cease to be deep and relatively quiet and they are faster and rockier and shallower, and you cannot use them for transportation.

So, up at the falls line in the old days you could take flatboats all the way up to where the old Black Creek Road crosses the Contentnea Creek, oh, about half a mile, something like that, east of 301. About where the railroad trestle crosses is where it begins to be shallow and rocky and never could be used for boats unless it was during a flood time when the water would have been exceedingly high, and, of course, you could pass over the rocks.

But, apparently, from around Stantonsburg on down, the creek was navigable to these flatboats, and they could transport their barrels of tar and turpentine and bales of cotton and so on, ship it on down to New Bern; and from there, of course, it was loaded on bigger vessels and went on up the coast to New England or down the coast to Bermuda.

But Stantonsburg, because it was the principal closest landing for the flatboats or barges, became the first town in what is now Wilson County, which was incorporated by the General Assembly. That was in 1817.

And it wasn't until 1849 that the town of Wilson was incorporated.

This business of navigation was very important to the people in the early days, and the larger streams were very useful since the roads were simply terrible. I don't know if you've heard that old story about how bad the roads were out in the eastern part of the state.

But this man was riding his horse along, and he came to this tremendous mud puddle. And he couldn't get by. There was a hat, seemingly, floating around in this mudhole. So, he got off his horse. It was a rather nice looking hat, and he started to fish it out. When he lifted the hat up with a stick, he saw there was a man's head there. And he was rather embarrassed. He said, "Well, this is a mighty big mud puddle."

"I'll say," said the man. "I'm standing in my horse's saddle."

It was no joke that a wheel would drop off down into a mudhole up to the axle. Even where there were causeways, that is, where dirt had been filled to give a certain high ground, it would drain. When you had causeways over these swamps, in bad weather they were terrifically soft.

And what they did there was to build corduroy roads. Are you familiar with corduroy roads?

Well, over these woods paths and maybe even the roads that had to pass over long swampy areas, they cut these little saplings and laid them side by side, just making a virtual "pole walk," and you could run your cart or wagon over that. It was horribly bumpy, but at least you didn't mire down and have to unload everything. And they called them the corduroy roads. Sort of a homemade thing.

And then it was 1850 or thereabouts that they formed the plank road company here in this area. They had already run some plank roads in the Piedmont. And, of course, we know that they were simply, for all practical purposes, a board fence lying flat on the ground, going mile after mile after mile.

They constructed one from Greenville to where the railroad crossing now is in Wilson. The fatal flaw to the plank road craze, and it was a craze at one time—everybody thought you could make a killing at it—was that by the end of seven years even your best oak, every single piece of it, had to be replaced.

If it had lasted longer, of course, it would have been just fine; but every single piece would have to be replaced by the end of seven years.

And the price that was charged—a penny or two cents . . . for a horse and rider or so much for a wagon or cart or a dozen hogs or what not—the price that you could charge simply would not repay the cost of replacement and leave anything for the stockholders.

And so the plank roads disappeared almost as quickly as they began. And this one, which was designed to go all the way to Raleigh, got to Wilson. It started from the Tar River in Greenville. And it crossed over everything in the way, over causeways and bridges, and brought it to the railroad in Wilson.

Now, the railroad was run in 1840, and I think it was about March 5, somewhere along there, that the first train ran all the way from Wilmington to Weldon. And at about 160¾ miles, that was the longest single piece of railroad track in the world at that time.

Now, getting back to roads and paths, the eastern part of the state, where they have so much sandy, loamy soil, and in the lowlands, particularly, these roads were simply terrible in wet weather.

That is why, for so long, those people didn't have coaches. The best thing to go in was a cart because a cart had only two wheels, and they were two big wheels. Tall, two-wheeled affairs. And it could go in a mudhole and pull out of it much better than anything else. A wagon with small wheels would get you in real trouble.

But even with a cart, sometimes you'd get in such a bad place that you'd have to unload a cart and get it out of the mud, then carry the stuff and reload it again, and go on.

During the Civil War, Wilson County, as well as the rest of eastern North Carolina, was grown up in forests with a few fields here and a few fields there, but just unimaginably woodsy, grown up, as compared to what you know at the present time. And so you'd travel a long way through the woods before you'd come to a little clearing. Not too much travel was done except on the post roads, the most important routes that ran north and south, east and west. The others, after all, didn't get too much attention.

A fellow, if he wanted to go to preaching or something like that, would go on horseback. And taking a wagon off, especially during wet weather, was something of a risk.

HUGH B. JOHNSTON, JR., 1913
Wilson County

Walking

I
think of Kipling's words
in regard
to my friend, Hermie.

Yes,
we would walk for miles
and
never
say
a word.

We were friends.

And
talking
would spoil
good tobacco.

LEE EDWIN KISER, D.C., 1898
Iredell County

Paths

There were paths everywhere. Now, the path Hermie and I would come from King on went right through those woods and across the creek down there, right south of those tobacco barns over there. And we'd split up at Slate's and I'd go north and he'd often come on over here. But we slept in the barn quite often. His daddy's barn or mine, one.

Why, we could walk those paths in our sleep . . . There was one right over yonder where we walked to Creason School.

On out there on the crest of that hill, it went to sleetin' one time and my feet slipped out from under me, and I went on down and I slid on all the way across the creek and stopped on the other side.

Didn't go in the creek. I just went right over it, I was going so fast. No, I don't know as the creek was frozen, but all that that I'd been traveling on was frozen. I was going at such a good speed.

LEE EDWIN KISER, D.C., 1898
Iredell County, speaking of his boyhood in Stokes

Fording the River

The mill was halfway between home and my Grandfather Phillips's. See, we'd go right by the mill and cross the Little Yadkin just below the dam. And, oh, it used to frighten me to death because the water would come up so close to the buggy, the axle of the wheel. And I'd close my eyes and hope we'd get across safely.

That's one of my earliest recollections. Going down to Grandma's. I always dreaded going across the Little Yadkin down there. 'Course, they wouldn't have gone in if they hadn't thought there was no danger. But there was one place that was kind of deep, and that always frightened me.

LOUISE PHILLIPS KISER, 1898
Iredell County

From Covered Wagons

When we got married and started out for ourselves, the first thing we bought was a one-horse wagon. It was covered. Yes, covered, with sheets and breakers. I made the sheets and breakers. The breaker was a sheet on top of the other sheet, but it wasn't quite as big. We called it a breaker. Yes, it kept you dry.

They was pulled real tight over the hoops, or the bows, and they turned the water. I put a drawstring in each end and pulled them down real tight. White "messic" [domestic]. Yes, they were white, and I sewed strips all around and hemmed them about that wide [measures on hand].

We put chairs inside to sit on. I always put a chair in for all that wanted them. Sometimes the children had rather sit on the floor. Then I put a quilt in, but mostly it was chairs.

And, oh, I just loved riding horses better than anything. My pappy bought me a gentle mule to ride, and that's what I went on, with my sidesaddle. I loved my sidesaddle, and I kept it even after I got married. I still had it when our house burned, and it burned, too. I wish I still had it. I wouldn't have taken nothing for it.

But I'm not through telling you about what we rode in. After our wagon, we got us a buggy, a big heavy-topped buggy. Then, as the children growed on, we got us a good surrey. Well, That was the best thing you ever rode in nearly. How were they shaped? Well, the buggy just came up around here, with a top on it. I can't hardly say just exactly. It had a banister come all around it.

And the buggy had one seat, but the surrey had two seats.

Did the surrey have a fringe on top? Well, no, I don't think so. But it had something like a curtain around the top, and a seat up here and one, then, back here, you see.

And then in 1920 we bought our first automobile, a two-seated Ford.

MINNIE LEE SPENCER, 1879
Stokes County

The Visitor

One of my brothers
who came back from the war [WWI],
he helped out one summer to keep that
upper mill open.
And it was rather lonely
up there for him.
He'd go and stay all week
and just come home on weekends.
And he told about this old gentleman,
one of the most interesting old characters
he'd ever seen.
He'd come and sit down at the mill, chat, talk.

And he'd say,
"Now, Mr. Phillips,
time was if they had a wagon,
people thought they were mighty lucky
if they had a wagon to ride in.
And then they got so they had buggies.
Fine buggies.
And after a while,
they got so they had buggies without the horses.
And now, they tell me,
the big 'uns are took to the aur!"

LOUISE PHILLIPS KISER, 1898
Iredell County

Eastern Cart

Now, the land plaster or fertilize was brought in down here, and we had to get our wagon down to pick it up. And, of course, it was rough at times because we had what is known as the River Hill here, quite a steep hill. And in those days it was dirt roads, and when it rained, you'd have the wagon wheels mired up in the mud so that you could only bring a small load up the hill. You'd have to bring part of it up the hill and unload and go and get some more.

I mean, suppose you were going to travel a distance. You might need 800 pounds of fertilizer. You'd go and get 400 pounds and bring it up and unload it. And that happened real often. 'Course, in those days, work didn't mean much. People didn't mind work. They expected it. They knew it. And they never thought anything about it.

In most parts of the country, they used a wagon. But I don't remember seeing the cart we used down here in other parts of the country. We used carts most of the time, I suppose because of the high wheels being needed in the swampy, spongy areas around here. It would not be as likely to stick. You only had two wheels to pull instead of four. And it was high and short. You'd balance the load on the cart.

And I'm sure some of the oldest settlers brought the idea of that kind of cart with them from the old countries. You know, this is the oldest part of the state because settlers came right down the river from Jamestown, right down this river. I mean this part was settled out of Jamestown. I suppose the way they came was by the Nottoway. They traveled on down and went into the Chowan and on down to Winton, and they went into the Sound.

And that was the way this part of the country was settled. Around 1623. They were in here pretty early. And that old cart has that history to it. And we'd see them on up, even fifteen or twenty years ago we'd still see them. With a mule hitched to them. We had a few wagons back in those early days, but not many. Most everything in this part of the country was the cart.

CHARLES L. REVELLE, SR., 1900
Hertford County

Ferry Across the Yadkin

And they run a ferry across the Yadkin River. My father, Augustine Eugene Conrad, did; and my grandfather before him. My grandfather owned all the land on one side, and my father owned the land on the other side.

Oh, yes. The ferry was there until 1916. Do you know what the ferry looked like? Well, it was a flatboat long enough for two wagons and horses to go in. They just drive in there on the boat, and they went from this side to the other. And then they had a big wire that run across the river. It was fastened on this side up above, on the tree top, or something like that, you know. And then on the other side, to the tree over there. And they had a

wire at each end of the boat to go up to the wire up above, from each end.

And then they had something about this long [demonstrates], with little wheels on it, to run on the big wire up there. And they could wind up one at one end, according to which way they was going; if they was going across the river, they'd wind up that one over yonder on the far end. And they'd leave the other one loose. And the boat would just set thataway, and it would push it on across the river.

And there was one time they had a chair onto the wire up yonder, and when the river got up, that chair could be used for one man to get across. The mailman had to go across. He had two places he had to get to across the river.

They charged about twenty-five cents for a wagon to go across, I think. And five cents to take a man across. The horses and mules went with the wagon. And you could go across with a buggy for about fifteen cents. And a horseback rider for about five cents.

Sometimes they'd have trouble with the river getting rough and the lines breaking. But they didn't break often.

ₗAnd there were times the river did freeze over. I never did see it, but I've heard tell of it. And the wagons would drive over on the ice.

They built the first bridge up there in 1916. They just had finished the bridge, and it come a big flood—the biggest I've ever seen. 1916. And the bridge was in pieces. One end of it wasn't fastened down. It was just against the end of the other side. And the water got up against the bridge, just enough to wash one section down. But that section hit against another section over here, and it couldn't go any farther. But if it had a-gone farther, it would have washed the whole bridge out. It was made out of wood, altogether wood.

EUGENE MOORE CONRAD, 1892
Forsyth County

Hoover Cart

Rubber tires on an old wagon.
Pulled it with a mule.
Hoover cart.
Well,
they didn't call it that other places,
just 'cause North Carolina
was Democratic,
and anything they could say against Hoover,
who was the smartest president we've had—
had more sense than all the rest of 'em

put together
since I was born in 1898.

That's the way they talked about him . . .

"Hoover Days, Hoover Days."

If they'd listened to Hoover,
we wouldn't be under all this debt
we've got now.
And our great-great-grandchildren
wouldn't be thinking what boobs we were
to put 'em in debt like that.

LEE EDWIN KISER, D.C., 1898
Iredell County

Early Train Travel

I had an uncle in Greensboro, and Mother took me on the train down there. And they had about two drivers on the side to steer it, like that. Big engine. They had a baggage car, and there might be a mail car combined—not over three cars.

And King's cabin was right over on the top of the hill up there. King married Elizabeth Kiser, and she was Jim Kiser's sister and Aunt Peggy Moore's sister. Margaret Kiser Moore, Hermie's grandmother, was her sister, too. And they had one child, and King's cabin up there is where they lived. And that was what King was named for. About a mile this side of where King is now. . . .

But my wife's granddaddy, David Nicholas Dalton, gave the railroad that ran from Fayetteville to Mount Airy, the Cape Fear, Yadkin Valley, I think it was—well, he gave 'em Dalton—that is, the place for the water tank. There was a post office and for the depot and all, and they had an agreement that they wouldn't build a railroad station between Rural Hall and Dalton.

But then it went into bankruptcy, or it changed names. Anyway, the new owners were no longer obligated by that. And so they built a depot at King and named it "King" for King's cabin, which was about one mile east of the present King. Right on top of the knoll.

And, incidentally, that's the highest point between Fayetteville and Mt. Airy, back up here at King's cabin. Right there at the top of the hill. I have heard 'em [the trains] when they'd just give a puff now and then. They just could make it over that hill.

Well, now, riding on that train, you'd get a little sooty. It was not air-conditioned. A few cinders. You'd get the smoke, the soot.

And they had a little old stove in the front of the car—and a toilet, too. And they had a sort of a gas light or acetylene light.

LEE EDWIN KISER, D.C., 1898
Iredell County, speaking of his boyhood in Stokes

The Ride

I'd run a mile
to get to ride a mile.
I'd hear this car coming,
you know.

Well, I'd have to run;
I'd have to go nearly a mile
before I could see it.
To the main road.
You could hear it coming a long way.

And I'd run a mile
to get to ride a mile.
I was born in 1902.

And these cars would come up there
once in a while.
It was very unusual.

Sometimes they would stop
and pick somebody up
and give 'em a ride along the road.
If they weren't already loaded.

It was wonderful!

Yes, it was!

CLEO ELAM, 1902
Cleveland County

Early Automobiles

The first automobile that ever I saw was in 1912 or '14. It was a T Model Ford. One of 'em. And I saw a Dodge. Mr. Will Slate had a Dodge car. It was a little bigger than a Ford, you know. Oh, it had oil lamps. It had headlights, but then it had oil lamps up near the windshield. Oh, your Grandpa Moore down here had one about like that. Lucian. But a Ford was about the smallest one there was.

Oh, I did see one they called a "motor buggy." Around 1909 or '10. Had high wheels on it, you know. About like a buggy that you hooked a horse to, but it had a motor in it. Down in the footboard, like. Some fellow, Leake, come up from Winston in one. And that was a curiosity, now, I'm telling you.

My dad bought an automobile in 1916. They had leather seats then and were made out of good steel. Why, there was more steel in two fenders then than there is on the whole body of a car now—the weight of it, I mean.

They were stout and strong. Why, you could run against a brick wall then.

Oh, yeah. The ladies wore dusters, a long thin coat, and a scarf over their hat then. My mother and sister had one to wear . . . you know, the roads were dusty then. And they'd wear these dusters to keep their clothes clean. They was washable. Like linen. And heavier than dress material, but wasn't real heavy. They called them dusters.

The automobiles had a top to 'em and curtains around. There were thin isinglass windows to look out.

Oh, that was the day!

LELIA F. BAKER, 1903
Stokes County

Route Directions

I had the general route marked out, but I had to ask in one place, one town, "How do I get to this place, this town?"

And oftentimes I'd get answers something like, "Well, you go down here and turn, right there by that barn, you turn right around the end of that barn and you go out there for, oh, a little piece, maybe a mile or two, and you come to a crossroads. You take that righthand road and go up that way and you find a bunch of cows," or something like that, you know. And you just kept on going and asking directions as you went. That was about as much direction as you'd get.

There were few routes marked. And the roads, well, they could have been improved. They were just roads—field roads, much of the time— you might be going between farms on field roads.

GERTRUDE M. KISER, 1897
Scotland County

11 STORIES AND LEGENDS

The heritage of North Carolina is enriched by the vast number of stories and legends that have originated among its people. Told around the family fireside, on the front porch in summer, or at the country store down the road, they have never failed to captivate the imagination of each successive generation. Being true to life as rural Carolinians have known it, these representative accounts date from as early as Revolutionary times.

What Grandfather Told Me

Grandfather's father
saw
the stars fall.

And
he told Grandfather
what
he
saw,

and
Grandfather told me.

You know,
the
stars
fell
November 13, 1833.

HUGH B. JOHNSTON, JR., 1913
Wilson County

The Time the Stars Fell

This was the time the eastern United States passed through the tail of Halley's Comet. And it was called, among the old folks, the "time the stars fell."

And I picked up two stories about it. One of them was this one that my grandfather told me. His father was born in 1818. Let's see, eight from thirteen is five, isn't it? Well, he was about fifteen years old. And in that day he lived about half a mile from here where there is just a field now, but in those days there was a house there. And the old walnut tree remained in the field until 1935, when it died and we cut it down. And that bench that you see there was made from some of the wood of that old walnut tree that stood in the yard of the Old Hilliard Thomas home, where Grandpa's father was born in 1818.

But anyway, the house stood there where there's just a plowed field now. And he went out on the back porch that particular night to get some water. They always kept some water on the water shelf with a dipper that everybody used. He went out to get some water, and he said it looked as though the fire was just literally raining from the sky, just like raindrops falling.

No, they didn't have the slightest idea about any comet.

Now, the other thing is in a book that belonged to Nathan Daniel, who was a merchant down at Stantonsburg at that time. The book is sitting up here on one of these shelves. His granddaughter gave it to me years ago. But on the flyleaf of the book he wrote, ''November 13, 1833. A wonder to mortal man as it regards the human body, the 13th day of November 1833 was the day that brought sum few individuals to pray that was said never trid to pray before in their life maid sum thing [think] that the world was going to be to an end—on the account of the stars shoting & blasing and fawling from the sky.''

See, they were ignorant people, and many thought the world was coming to an end. And, seemingly, the tail of the comet was truly a fiery

one. It didn't ignite anything so far as I know, but it was literally a rain of fire.

Yes, apparently, the little bits were burning up in the atmosphere, so that when they struck the ground, there was no fire there to set anything on fire. Otherwise, there would have been a terrible conflagration.

HUGH B. JOHNSTON, JR., 1913
Wilson County

Before Aspirin

And when my husband was just starting out as a doctor, he was trying to get practice. They used to try, to have to try, you know. And they called him and he went to see this little old lady. He gave her some capsules. And they used to carry their medicine with them. They had a bag, and it was full of soda pills, a lot of it was, you know, to make you think they were giving you something. They didn't have aspirin. That was before aspirin; can you imagine? Anyway, they'd have a few pills. Well, he gave her some capsules. And you know how they're put together.

Well, her daughter kept saying, "Here, Ma, take your medicine. Here's your medicine." She

wouldn't take it. And she wouldn't take it. Finally, the daughter asked, "Why don't you want to take it?"

And the little old lady said, "I'm afraid to take them there cartridges. Why, I'd blow up in a minute!"

FRANCES C. COLE, 1890
Buncombe County

Mousehole Hunting

Now, I can tell you a worse tale than that, though. My grandpa and his two little brothers, when they were small and the chestnuts had all fell, you know, and got gone, they went a-mousehole huntin', they called it. And they found an old snag [hollow tree limb] torn all to pieces. Chestnuts just scattered on the ground.

They called it a mousehole or a ground squirrel, one. Either one packs 'em in snags. They used to gather the chestnuts when they fell and put 'em in an old snag. They'd pack a layer of dirt and a layer of chestnuts. You know, ground squirrels would.

And so they went, one foggy day; these three little boys took their basket and their axe and they come on this old snag tore all to pieces and the ground just speckled with chestnuts. And they turned into picking up chestnuts just as hard as they could. My grandfather and his two brothers, now.

And they picked up a while, and something screamed at them from over on the other ridge, and it scared 'em—you know, little boys—but they picked up that much harder. Toreckly, it got a little closer and screamed at 'em again. They just kept on, and, in a little bit it come closer and screamed again. And the little fellers left—got scared.

And they went home and told what had happened to 'em. And their parents told 'em if they hadn't left, it would have torn them all to pieces.

It was a panther. Yeah! He'd tore that old snag up to get the chestnuts himself, and they got so close on him it scared him. And he'd run off and left them. But when they went to picking up his chestnuts, he wasn't satisfied

MARTHA TOLIVER ABSHER, 1878
Alleghany County

The Lost Pot

Right down the river here apiece, there's a Shallowford Road that goes across the river there, just above where the Shallow Ford used to be. And Cornwallis came up from down beside the river, came up the road there, and crossed over at the Shallow Ford with his army. The river was up, down below there, and he had to come up there to cross it.

And there's some people over here now on the other side of the river who are descendants of a man who got away then. He lost his pot. What he cooked in, you know? They all had their own old pots, and he lost his off his horse in coming across the river. When they got on this side, he got off his horse and went back and waded out in the river and picked up his pot and got it.

And now there's a road up in there on the other side of the river, and that's where this man went and settled there. He just took off and deserted the army.

And there's a man down here at West Bend that told me once that he had that same pot. I don't know whether he does or not, but that's what he told me.

EUGENE MOORE CONRAD, 1892
Forsyth County

Cornwallis and the Cow

Cornwallis come on up by here and crossed Conrad Road out yonder, I reckon about three-quarters of a mile it was from here. And he went on by Grapevine Schoolhouse and went on up to Brookstown Church and went on to Bethania and up thataway. But anyway, that was always the way I was told he went with his army.

And some of his soldiers was hunting up something to eat, you know, and they got a cow over there from my great-great grandma. She lived there by the old mill. Anyway, these fellows went by there and got the cow and went on up the road, and she followed them. And said, she told them she had to have that cow back. But they wouldn't give it to her. And when they got up to where Cornwallis was, he let her have it.

EUGENE MOORE CONRAD, 1892
Forsyth County

Saved by a Petticoat

The John Martin who built the Rock House was my great-great-grandfather. Now, I've heard my grandmother say—course, I was just a young fellow then—that this girl, this daughter of John Martin, was captured by the Tories and taken to the Tory's Den over there on the side of the mountain. And she said you could see the Rock House from the Tory's Den.

And that girl took her petticoat off and waved it, right thisaway. And her daddy saw it. And he got some people to go with him over there to get her.

And the Tories had found out that he was a-coming so they took her and went on down towards Danbury. But she would tear off a piece of her clothes and throw 'em down every once in a while. And so he traced her. And he found her right over there where the river makes a bend there somewhere about Danbury. I've been to the place.

Now, I just heard about this when I was just a young boy. And he caught up with her down there and captured some of the Tories who had her, I think. But I don't know which one of the girls she was.

EUGENE MOORE CONRAD, 1892
Forsyth County

Osborne

Looting by the Yankees

During the time of the War Between the States, my mother was living then. She was nine years old. And the army went right through here. They camped just below my grandfather's house.

And my mother's people—there were thirteen of them, I think, quite a crowd—and up until that time they'd all had a college education. 'Course, after that, there wasn't anything. Uncle Cal and my mother came along close together. And they had a lot of goose eggs. So they took and hid the goose eggs on the pillars under the house. You could slip them up under there.

And the soldiers found every one of their goose eggs. They'd take their spears, you know, and go around and find where they'd buried their hams and things.

But the worst thing about that, I suppose, was that my grandfather had the boys in the family. They were big strong fellows, but they were not old enough to go to the war. But he took them and some of the slaves and horses and mules and things way down in the dark swamp.

And my grandmother would always take their meals to them. Had a trustee woman to go with her, one of the slaves. But in the meantime, the Yankees bribed one of the slaves to tell them, and he told where to find 'em. And the last they saw of him, he was on one of the horses riding off. And the Yankees took every mule and horse they had and burned up the feed. They didn't hurt my grandfather and the boys. They just took everything they had.

MARY C. MC KINNON, 1886
Scotland County

They Killed the Money

And that's when they had that awful time. You see, Grandpa was a Democrat, and the Republicans hated the Democrats. That's the way it was.

And they treated him and Uncle John awful bad when they ended up the war, you know. They took everything they had, except land.

Killed the money. All the money they had, you see, they killed it. They couldn't do anything with it. It was Confederate, you know. And left them with nothing. They just might' near had nothing to eat. They even stole the meat, everything they had. They drove all the cattle off, all the mules and horses. Hogs. A gang would follow and drive the animals all off. Just took them away from you and took them off.

Now, they had a place up here somewhere that they took all the animals to. And the law found it out and they went to taking and giving the stuff back to the people.

So one day my Granddaddy Grogan went up there because they had taken his mule. He'd found out the place where it was, and he went to get his mule. They asked him all about it, what color it was, and all. He told them it was a yellow mule and that one time when the saddle was on it, it had hurt a little place on its back and made a sore. So when the hair had come back in that spot, it was white.

And he said that while he was talking, up come a man on his mule. And he just went over and took the saddle off and showed him that little white spot. It was his mule, so they gave it to him, and he brought it on back home.

MINNIE LEE SPENCER, 1879
Stokes County

Collecting Food

My grandfather, Hugh Archie Campbell, was crippled. He was of the age to go into the army, Confederate Army. But, due to his physical condition, he was rejected. And during the war he and this Mr. McMillan, I think his name was, collected tithes from farmers all around through Robeson County. A tenth of what they had. They called it a tithe, where there was a tenth of what they could spare.

It was either food—dried food—dried beans and fruit and things that the soldiers could eat. Or, I think they gathered and sent some fatback and some fodder and things for the horses. And they went from farm to farm and collected it, and it was all sent in to a central place. They carried a wagonload when they'd get it together.

MARGIE CAMPBELL, 1902
Scotland County

Brothers in Battle

In the family my grandfather's mother's twin brother, George Washington Woodard, was in the Confederate Army, and he became sick with the, probably, dysentery that killed so many Southern boys, and they put him in the hospital at Staunton, Virginia. And he died in the hospital there.

My Grandmother Johnston was a Dillard, and she had four brothers who were born and reared there in the vicinity of Rocky Mount, and they went into the Confederate Army. Three of those boys surrendered under Lee at Appomattox Courthouse. Went all through the war, three of them.

And the other one was gravely wounded, but survived. But the nature of his wound was unusual. At the Battle of Warwick's Creek, they were charging against the Yankees who were posted on higher ground on the far side of the creek. And, as they were crossing the creek, Uncle John took a Minie ball in the head. Large ball, I guess a .58 caliber. And he fell face down in the creek.

Uncle Ed Dillard was right beside him. And he reached down and grabbed him by his shirt and suspenders and dragged him out of the water and left him under the shade of a little pine tree as he went on with the rest of the boys charging the Yankees. Well, the Yankees broke and ran.

But, Uncle Ed, as he told the story, said that he fixed his mind, more or less, on one particular Yankee that he thought was the one that had fired the shot that took Uncle John in the head. And so when they got up the bank and the Yankees were running, he shot this fellow right where his suspenders crossed in the back. And the fellow fell down and, of course, died. He intimated that he did, as he passed, quickly run his hand through his [the fallen Yankee's] pockets and strike whatever greenbacks he had in his pockets, then went on with the charge. But that was a customary thing in those days, to take money off the fallen enemy that he wasn't going to be able to use any more.

But he came back after the charge was stopped, and he found that Uncle John was still breathing. The ball had struck him right about the hairline in the middle of the forehead. And it passed into his brain somewhere, and there was a little blood oozing from the wound. But Uncle John was still breathing.

So Uncle Ed and a friend took him to a first-aid station there, and they poured whiskey over it or whatever they did to cleanse the wound as well as they could. They didn't dare do any delving in there because in those days you just didn't do that. They didn't know enough about it. So they dressed the wound. And, of course, Uncle John was unconscious, but he still was breathing.

So, after two or three days when they moved all the wounded down to Richmond to the hospital, they moved him. And so he was in the hospital there at Richmond, I think, maybe for a couple of weeks. And he finally recovered consciousness. The place healed over. They did not put a plate in his head—the place just healed over, leaving a depression.

And so he lived until 1905 with that Yankee ball embedded down in his brain. In his last years, I understand, at times, especially in heavy, damp weather, he had terrible headaches.

Now, in retrospect, the thing that undoubtedly saved him was that the bullet was not traveling at a high rate of speed. But it was enough to penetrate the bone, and it passed between the two lobes. That had to be the explanation for it. It passed between the two lobes of the brain and lodged under there without any major rupturing of anything. And, as luck would have it, he did not have gangrene set in, which in many cases caused the fellows to have their legs amputated, and in that sort of a wound there would have been nothing to amputate. But he didn't have any infection to set in.

And he survived, married, and had three children. Two girls never married; a son married in later life, never had any children, and died, and so that line is extinct.

HUGH B. JOHNSTON, JR., 1913
Wilson County

Cape Lookout Lighthouse Stories

Now, most of that land around Cape Lookout Lighthouse was marshy. You see, that lighthouse was built in 1857, before the Civil War. It's 187 feet tall, and it had a 350,000-candlepower light in it. The reflector and the prisms were made in France in 1839 or '40, something like that, because at that time we weren't far enough along to make anything like that. And those things looked like diamonds. We used to have to shine them occasionally. I never did; one of the other fellows used to. Well, I did one time.

That lighthouse . . . well, I wish I could remember the exact dimensions . . . but the walls are at least twelve feet thick. You walk into a door and go through a wall that thick. Solid brick. Inside it's straight. Outside, it tapers off toward the top. Up near the top, it's only about three or four bricks thick. See? Well, inside you have a

hollow center, a metal column with a door in it. And attached to that column are the stairs that go around and around till you get to the top.

Well, the reason that thing was hollow: back in the 1800s, they used to have a weight mechanism, like a weight on a grandfather clock, you know. And they had this huge crank. And every day the lighthouse keeper would have to go up there and put his oil in his lamp. And around his lamp he had this disc that would make this character as it would turn slowly. It had this big slot and then a little slot, a big slot and a little slot. It's a letter C, in the International Morse Code. And when I was there, we transmitted the letter C over the radio to identify us, "Cape Lookout." But back then they used the discs.

And they were on a drive mechanism operated by weights. Well, he'd go up and fill his container full of oil. Then he'd take his crank and engage it into this thing and he'd crank his weight all the way up to the top. Then, when the sunset came, he's go up and release this lever and the thing would start turning. And the weight would keep it turning, flashing out the letter C, out to the ships at sea. It was all oil then.

Now, another thing about this lighthouse—there used to be some keepers there and they got onto this idea and they got one of these ponies.

Now, that's a pretty terrible job, you know, carrying a huge can of oil up all those stairs. That's 187 feet, a lot of steps, an awful climb. So they rigged them up a block and tackle, and they'd hook their oil can to the rope and they'd get their pony on the other end of it and hook him up and lead him out. That way they'd run their oil can up to the top where they could get it off, see? The pony would walk straight from the lighthouse and be pulling the oil can up. And that's the way they hoisted their oil.

JOHN D. COBLE, 1912
Former lighthouse keeper, Cape Lookout,
now living in Stokes County

The Banker Ponies

Well, now you've heard of the banker ponies? Well, there were not only ponies—there were cows and sheep, too . . . and they just ran loose on the banks; nobody looked after them.

Now, a funny thing about it. This island [Harkers] was about twenty-two miles long, and they would migrate from one end to the other. Well, they'd go up to the north end, and by the time they'd get back, there'd be a little bit more

grass, see? That would give it time to grow, and they'd just work back and forth, like that.

The cows would go right along with them. And so would the sheep. Generally, they kind of stayed together. You might look out there one day and see them about five miles up the beach; then the next day they'd be about two miles. The next day they'd pass you. But they had no shelter out there, no protection. Sometimes they might get behind a few sand dunes, but they were pretty well conditioned to the weather.

But one of the most fascinating things: if you'll stop and think about it, a horse can dig. Now, those banker ponies, there was no one to look after them and trim their hoofs. You know, they would grow like a toenail or a fingernail. And some of them would curl up, and they would actually split. And they would get sore feet and eventually, sometimes, they would get an infection and die. And occasionally they'd break off and they'd be all right. But anyway, when they'd get thirsty, those horses would start digging right out on the high part of the beach there someplace. And maybe there'd be one here and one here and three or four over there, scattered around, and just like a dog—clawing with their front paws, and pretty soon their belly would be on the ground and they'd be down in the hole.

And you'd see him get through, and another one would go down there and drink his fill. Well, all the time, the horses would drink first; the cows and the sheep have split hoofs, so they can't dig, and they'd just stand around and wait. When the horses got through, the cows would start drinking, and then when the cows got through, the sheep would drink. Then they'd migrate on down the beach. And the next day they'd start digging more holes. Well, the wind and the tide and everything would come in and cover them up.

Now, another fascinating thing about those animals: at times the mosquitoes were terrible out there. Usually we had wind, but you get down to the evening when the wind has calmed down, and in that marsh grass where it's a little mucky and muddy, there's millions of these little black mosquitoes, we call them. O. K. They would get so bad that the poor animals just couldn't get away from them. There was no relief in sight. And you know what they did? They'd go out in the Cape Lookout bight, in the salt water, and they'd go just as far out as they could to keep their nose and eyes above water. And, as the tide would go out, they'd keep going out a little farther; and as the tide would come in, they'd gradually keep coming in,

just enough to keep their nose and eyes so they could breathe. And you could look out there on an evening sometimes and see five or six hundred heads just up above the water.

We had one boy at the Navy station, that, one of those cows was so pretty, and she had a calf, and she had a right nice-sized udder on her, and he decided, "Well, that cow's so pretty, I'm going to get some feed and start feeding that thing and milking her." 'Cause he had a kid or two. His name was Dabney, and I'll never forget him as long as I live. He was from Alabama. And he caught this old cow and she was a pretty thing, and he bought some hay and he bought some cow feed. Brought it over there and started feeding that cow like a regular cow.

And the food was so rich the cow died in about two weeks. Just couldn't stand it.

JOHN D. COBLE, 1912
Former lighthouse keeper, Cape Lookout,
now living in Stokes County

New Holland

Back about the turn of the century, there was a Russian agricultural expert visiting this country. A group of wealthy people from up north brought him down to this area around Lake

Mattamuskeet. He stayed several days and analyzed the soil. That is, the soil on the bottom of the lake.

And he told those people that the soil there was so rich that if some way they could drain that lake, then they could raise any crop or plant which would grow in this climate for a hundred years without any fertilizer.

So these money people, they got interested, and they had some engineering work done. And they decided they would try it. Now, this lake is around seven or eight miles wide and about fifteen miles long. There's not a place in it that's over three feet deep. So they decided they would try to pump it dry. Now, this was a huge engineering project. If I remember this correctly, they built a huge pumping station on the south side of the lake; you can see it there now. And I believe there were about five canals running from the lake. They, maybe, were fifty or sixty feet wide, or maybe thirty or forty. They cut across all of them with the common canal, joining all of them. And right there they put the pumping station.

And they put in these huge commercial pumps. Then they had to dig a canal from there to the salt water, which was a mammoth project. And so they got the thing completed and started pumping, and they pumped the water out.

And where the lake is now, they built a little town, and they called it New Holland. And they had drugstores and a blacksmith shop and several homes. And that was right where the water is now. And they had quite a little village, post office, telegraph station. And Dutch people lived there and raised bulbs. They had decided that was the best thing to do with it. And they shipped a lot of those bulbs out, you see. At that time I was working in Wilmington at the telegraph station, and I remember seeing a lot of those orders being relayed.

And it all went on for I don't know how many years. And it was successful, but they had to work all the time to keep the water down. Finally, the water started gaining on them. And they did everything they possibly could, and eventually they had to abandon their village.

And there went their town. And they finally moved a few of their houses up near the pumping station. And the game wardens, that's their quarters. And the lake is there today, as you see it on the map. The pumping station they've converted into a hotel. And they had a huge chimney, from the boiler rooms, you know, they had this huge chimney. So what they did to decorate it, they made it look like a lighthouse.

The last time I was there, it was very

attractive. Now this lady innkeeper comes into my story, since she was there and asked me if I would like to know how the lake was originally formed. It makes a cute little story, anyway. I don't know how factual it is; it could be the truth, as far as I know.

JOHN D. COBLE, 1912
Former lighthouse keeper, Cape Lookout,
now living in Stokes County

On the Ferry

Yes 'm,
on the ferry
we get 'em all.

Comin' through here
from
all over
the world.

Sights
and
wonders . . .

We get 'em all . . .

CAPTAIN FLOYD DANIELS
of The Pamlico, *ferry between*
Cedar Island and Ocracoke, 1920
Carteret County

Ocracoke Stories

Capt. Garrish: Now you've heard of the *Carroll A. Deering*? Well, we can remember some of the people who boarded it. We lived here and knew some of them. 'Course they're dead now.

One of the men who boarded it was at the Coast Guard station, and I talked to him.

He said it was a pretty day, and they went aboard the vessel almost immediately after they sighted it. It was so pretty that you could see fourteen miles—thirteen or fourteen miles— 'cause this is where the vessel was ashore. It wasn't ashore on the beach. It was ashore on Diamond Shoals. It couldn't have been bad weather that caused it.

And when they got to the vessel, it was abandoned. The sails were up on it. And the remains of a meal was left on the stove and the table. Everything, apparently, was in order. This happened within our lifetime—1921. I can remember. Parts of the vessel later came on Ocracoke here. A storm moved parts of it here onto the beach. Then, in 1955, another storm moved it off of the beach and up to Hatteras. Today, part of it is laying in front of the Texaco filling station at Hatteras. It's a capstan, is what it is, a winch.

You see, the reason it couldn't be moved when it was found right at first—once a vessel runs aground, it's almost impossible to ever get it off. At that time we didn't have powerful tugboats like we have today. Today they could have possibly got that vessel.

'Course, Diamond Shoals is supposed to be quicksand. This is called the graveyard of the Atlantic, you know. We've had a lot of vessels come ashore on Ocracoke Beach since we can remember. I can remember at least four four-masted sailing vessels. They were loaded with lumber, usually.

The tides make it worse. You take a heavy wind like this; now this is what gets your sea up. And the forces of your sea . . . you wouldn't think so, but the forces of the sea will break up steel vessels. With waves just pounding on them, they're breakable.

One of the vessels, course I don't remember this one—my grandmother told me about it—the *Pioneer*—this was a sailing ship, or a combination sailing and steam ship. It came ashore in 1890, or somewhere around there, and it was loaded with general cargo. It had everything: boots, clothing, lumber, just general cargo. It broke up on Ocracoke beach. And then these people would go beachcombing. It was all right to do that if the ship was breaking up and everything was just floating around.

But this vessel, like I said, the folks went out to find what they could find. All kinds of stuff. They had lots of food, huge cabbage, coconuts. And this was in early December.

And then, there was a banana ship that came ashore. Steamship. This belonged to the United States Fruit Lines. This was a steamship line that went into the West Indies and brought back bananas. This thing was loaded with in the thousands of bunches of bananas that they were bringing. And they floated. Oh, yes! And later they freed that vessel, too. But they had to unload the ship. Now, everybody along here who had a small boat went out and loaded up their boats, alongside the ship. Then, when everybody got all they wanted, then they just threw them overboard. And the beach was just littered with bananas. Fifteen miles, there was bananas up and down the beach.

Mrs. Garrish: All the kids took bananas to school. I remember—there was seven of us children. And my father had the whole upstairs hanging with bunches of bananas. And all through the night and in the morning when we woke up, we was getting bananas and throwing them at one another. That's one of the things I remember. I was about thirteen or fourteen. Yes, my father had a boat, and he loaded it and brought them home. We had bananas fixed every way.

Capt. Garrish: Now, back to the *Carroll A. Deering*, I remember hearing that this vessel, when it passed *Frying Pan Lightship*, now this was about seventy-five or eighty miles south of here, the vessel was apparently sailing then at random. It wasn't under control. Now, you see, off the coast of North Carolina, *Frying Pan* is down here, but Diamond Shoals is thirteen miles off out here, out to sea, like a jut of land sticking out there. But I believe they said that about one day south of *Frying Pan* the crew had been on it, because there had been an entry in their log. So it happened between there and here. That was about a day and a half. And it was late, too. You know, it was on its maiden voyage. Brand new ship. It had left up north, coming down south and was on its return trip.

Mrs. Garrish: My father always said that the people here thought that whatever happened, it was sudden, because they didn't write anything in their log. Had it been something they'd had a little trouble with, coming along, someone would have taken time to log it.

And there was a cat, too. He was brought to the island, and I had one of the kittens from that cat. My father brought it home, and it was a Maltese. There were lots of those cats all up and down the Outer Banks, all from that cat. I know the woman who had it, and she gave my father one of the kittens.

Capt. Garrish: Somebody around here told us the other day they had a bed off that boat. Now, I wonder who that was?

Now, when things were washed ashore, the natives would all gather round and have a vendue. But they called it a "wandue." They pronounce the v like a w. And that was when they got together and auctioned off all the things.

Talking about the *Pioneer*, some of these people who went to the *Pioneer* to see what they could find. . . . well, my grandmother used to say that my grandfather and his buddy they went beachcombing, too. And they found a bottle of rum. So they didn't get home with much, but they had a big time of it.

And another part of this was, the neigh-bors, they were constantly swapping things they would find. For instance, if I found a shirt that wouldn't fit me, I'd find somebody it would fit. And swap, yeah.

And one boy, supposed to be a young fellow—I'm sure this is not all so. I heard it, and I added to it.—Well, while he was beachcombing, he found a pair of shoes. Now, all the shoes he had prior to this were hand-me-downs from his brother. So when he got home, he was happy to have a pair of shoes. But it was pointed out by his parents that one of his shoes was a number eight and the other was a number eleven. And both of them fitted the left foot!

Mrs. Garrish: There was four homes on this island that I know of, that the framing was built of the timbers off of the *Ida Lawrence* that came ashore here a long time ago. My father's was one of them. All those homes are old. My father's, I'd say that was seventy-five years old.

This one we're living in here was built of old ship timbers, too. It's about a hundred years old. We bought it already built. You can go down underneath it now and see those big old beams that came off the ship. We had the whole thing raised up two feet when we got it to keep the water out during times of storms.

And my dining-room table, setting right in here in the next room, came off a ship. It was a big long table when my father got it, but it's been shortened and refinished. I can show you where the holes were in each corner. You see, they had to run a rope through those holes to tie it down on the ship so it wouldn't go sliding all around. We had the holes plugged, but you can still see where they were.

My family was the Ballances. I don't know how long we've been here, but my grandfather could remember his grandfather being here. And my grandfather was ninety-four.

I've heard my grandmother say she can remember when Ocracoke and Hatteras was joined together and was all one. And they had this storm that came in July, and it cut this inlet. And my grandmother always spoke of it as the "July Galey." Instead of the "July Gale," they called it the "July Galey." Why that, I don't know. That was long before our time.

Another bad storm was in 1899. I've heard my father tell about this one. He and about five or six other fishermen were stranded down on what we here call the other end of the island; we call it "down below." But they were on this high hill and they had a skiff with a canvas over it. That's all they had. And they said everything around them drowned. The cattle, the horses, whatever was there. And, of course, some of them were young boys, quite disturbed. And my father wasn't very old. He said afterward, after the tide went down, that they had a lot of washouts and what-have-you. And he remembered coming home, and my grandmother had a kitchen that was built out away from the house—you know, older people built their kitchens away—and he said when he opened the door and walked in—they had gone to a neighbor's house that was up higher—that the mud was so deep on the kitchen floor that he slipped and fell flat of his back and he fainted. He said from hunger, mostly, because he had been out there three days.

He wouldn't have been down below, none of them would have, but they didn't have warnings of storms then like they do now. They didn't know it was coming up. My father was the last survivor of the crew that was there. They're all gone now.

CAPTAIN IRVING GARRISH, 1916
ELSIE BALLANCE GARRISH, 1915
Ocracoke Island, Hyde County

Sturgeon in the Chowan

In these fisheries down here the sturgeon, well, they didn't like 'em because they probably tore the net to pieces. They were a big fish. Sometimes, I think I remember hearing my grandfather say, they could be as long as six feet. This was a terrible big whale in these waters up here and with the herring.

But they would sell the meat. They would cut 'em up and sell 'em by the pound. But the roe, that's what they now use for caviar, well, they didn't do anything with it back then except to throw it out, and the chickens and ducks would thoroughly enjoy it.

These are stories that my grandfather told me. And around 1900 he was in his heyday.

LOUISE V. BOONE, 1922
Hertford County

Rough Weather Makes Good Timber

The house was built in '98,
prior to my arrival.
And a big maple tree
at the northeast corner of the porch
was run over and buried lots of times
by wagons moving in material to build the house.
And the other maples
what Daddy had planted,
they had no trouble atall.
But they all died
and this one lived that had such rough treatment.

And there's a saying,
"Rough weather makes good timber."

It may be
that the trouble with folks today
is
that they're raised like hothouse flowers,
and
they don't have much to go on
at the end.

LEE EDWIN KISER, D.C., 1898
Iredell County

The Authors

Patsy Moore Ginns has taught school in North Carolina, South Carolina, and Alaska, and has won awards for her short stories and children's poetry. She lives in King, Stokes County, North Carolina—on the same farm where her father was born.

J. L. Osborne, Jr., a native of Lexington, North Carolina, and a professional engineer, is well known for his pen-and-ink drawings of rural North Carolina scenes.